BEAT MULTIPLE DECK BLACKJACK

LEARN HOW TO BEAT MULTIPLE DECK GAMES WITHOUT COUNTING CARDS!

BEAT MULTIPLE DECK BLACKJACK

LEARN HOW TO BEAT MULTIPLE DECK GAMES WITHOUT COUNTING CARDS!

MARTEN JENSEN

CARDOZA PUBLISHING

ACKNOWLEDGMENT

To my dear wife DeAnna, whose astute suggestions and skillful manuscript editing helped make this a better book.

ABOUT THE AUTHOR

Marten Jensen, the "Doctor of Gambling," is one of the foremost authorities of gambling in the world. An expert on all the casino games, Jensen is also the author of six books on beating the casinos, all published by Cardoza Publishing.

Great Cardoza Publishing Books by Marten Jensen
Secrets of the New Casino Games
Secrets of Winning Roulette
Video Poker & Slots for the Winner
Beat the Slots
Beat Multiple Deck Blackjack
Beat the Craps Table

Cardoza Publishing is the largest gaming and gambling publisher in the world with a library of more than 200 up-to-date and easy-to-read books and strategies. These authoritative works are written by the top experts in their fields and with more than 10,000,000 books in print, represent the best-selling and most popular gaming books anywhere.

CARDOZA PUBLISHING

P.O. Box 98115, Las Vegas, NV 89193
Toll-Free Phone (800)577-WINS
email: cardozabooks@aol.com
www.cardozabooks.com

TABLE OF CONTENTS

1

Anyone can win money playing blackjack! Wait–don't you have to be able to count cards in order to win? Not necessarily! If you're the kind of player who would like to win consistently without having to count cards, this book is for you. In fact, the techniques described in the following pages are the same ones used by professional players when they are not counting.

Yes, professionals do, at times, play without counting for various reasons: it may be because the heat is on, or they are part of a team, or they are just relaxing their brain (counting is mentally strenuous). Even when they are not counting, however, they seem to be winning most of the time.

Blackjack is a very simple game to play. That is, it is an easy game to learn—all you have to do is try to get closer to a total count of 21 than the dealer, without going over. The tough part is knowing how to do this in a manner that will maximize your chance of winning the money.

Sometimes it is better to stand on a low total, and sometimes it is better to risk going bust by hitting a higher total. Sometimes it is better to double down, and sometimes it is better to hit. Sometimes it is better to split a pair, and sometimes it is better not to. This book will tell you exactly which actions will minimize the house edge and maximize your profits.

WHY THIS BOOK IS DIFFERENT

The bookstores carry many books on how to play black-jack. So what does this book offer that the others don't? Most books fall into one of two categories: they either oversimplify the game for rank beginners, or they describe complex and involved card counting methods for very advanced and professional players.

Beat Multiple Deck Blackjack covers the subject of blackjack playing strategy thoroughly without getting into the complexities of card counting systems. It is designed for novices and advanced players who want to play as well as they can without the mental strain of counting cards. It will teach those recreational players how to play their hands in the best way possible to win money.

In addition to the full-blown computer-derived basic playing strategy for the most advanced players, it also contains simplified versions of that strategy so that novice players can get a running start without a whole lot of memorization.

This book has another feature not found in most other blackjack books. There is no chitchat, not a single personal anecdote, and no gambling stories. It is solidly packed with useful data, facts, and the very best playing information. You will find none of the extraneous material that is included in most gambling books.

INTRODUCTION

The primary emphasis of this book is on the multiple deck games that have become the mainstay of casino blackjack. Those casinos that still offer them, are slowly changing the rules for single-deck hand-dealt games, making them harder to beat. So much so that when you do find a good single- or double-deck game, it is almost impossible to get a seat at the table. In my opinion, the recreational gambler can do just fine at multiple deck games by playing according to the basic strategy recommendations in this book.

In addition to providing the very best playing strategy, this book has some additional features. All the major side bets offered at some blackjack tables are fully described and evaluated. Complete strategy charts are provided for several modified blackjack games such as Double Exposure, Spanish 21, and Super Fun 21. There is also a complete chapter devoted to the playing strategy for private home games.

The major strategies in this book were devised and tested by the most respected specialists in the field. My special thanks to mathematical geniuses Michael Shackleford (The Wizard of Odds) and Stanley Wong for allowing me to publish their work. I would also like to acknowledge the late Julian Braun and the late Lenny Frome for their major contributions to the gambling knowledge base, which I have freely tapped.

Everyone wants to be a winner. Now you can be one, too. By carefully reading this book you can learn how to beat the multiple deck blackjack games, and have fun at the same time.

2

BLACKJACK FUNDAMENTALS

If you expect to beat casino blackjack without counting cards, it goes without saying that you need to know and understand the game in as much depth as possible. Before jumping over to the strategy tables in the later chapters, it would be time well spent to first absorb these early chapters, especially if you are a beginner or novice. If you are a more experienced player, at least review the material because I guarantee you will learn *something*.

OBJECT OF THE GAME

Once all the players have placed their bets, the game begins when the dealer distributes two cards to each player. In a multiple deck game, the players' cards are always dealt face-up. The dealer also gives herself two cards, one face-down and one face-up. Each player, in turn, is then given the opportunity to take additional cards, one at a time. Players may also exercise other options, such as splitting pairs and doubling down, all of which will be thoroughly explained later.

The main goal for the player is to *beat the dealer*. This can be done in two ways. The first is to attain a total count higher than the dealer's hand without exceeding 21 (called **busting**). The second is to keep the hand alive by staying under 21, in the hope that the dealer will bust and lose by default.

Since the dealer plays her hand last, the only clue players have for making their playing decisions is the dealer's upcard. In conjunction with the first two cards dealt to the player, the value of the dealer's upcard is the major basis for good playing strategy.

Sometimes the players' cards are dealt face down, but this is only done in single- and double-deck hand-dealt games—and, today, such games are in the minority. Blackjack games in most American casinos as well as in the rest of the world use four to eight decks of cards, all shuffled together and dealt from a shoe (see p. 15). Unless otherwise mentioned, the advice and strategies given in this book are for those multiple deck games.

THE EQUIPMENT
The implements used for playing blackjack in a casino are pretty basic. They include a half-moon table with stools for the players, several decks of cards, a dealing shoe, and a supply of casino chips. These items are described below.

The Playing Table
Blackjack is played on a felt-covered table that is roughly semicircular in shape with six or seven player positions around the curved side (see illustration). The dealer stands at the flat side with a chip rack directly in front of her and a card-dealing shoe to her left. To the dealer's immediate right is a slot in the tabletop leading to a drop box. Whenever the dealer accepts cash from a player in

exchange for casino chips, the cash is pushed into the drop box. Further to the dealer's right is a discard tray where the dealer deposits out-of-play cards that she has collected from the table.

Typical Blackjack Table

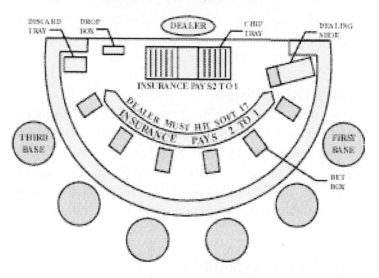

At each player position is a betting spot in the shape of a rectangle or a circle. This is where the player's initial bet is placed before the first two cards are dealt. During a player's turn, additional bets may be placed alongside the original bet when splitting pairs or doubling down.

The first player seat to the left of the dealer is called **first base**. This spot is the first hand dealt in a round of play. The last seat to the dealer's right is called the **anchor position**, and is also referred to as **third base**. It is the last player hand dealt in a round. The felt surface of the table has two or three basic game rules imprinted on it.

The most common rule is: *Dealer must draw to 16 and stand on all 17s.* In some games (sometimes in the same casino), this rule is modified to read: *Dealer must hit soft 17.*

A second rule that appears on almost all tabletops is: *Insurance pays 2 to 1.* Some tables display a third rule: *Blackjack pays 3 to 2.* If a natural does not pay 3 to 2, there will almost always be a sign to that effect.

The Dealing Shoe
Most blackjack games use four, six, or eight decks of cards, which are dealt from a **dealing shoe**. The shoe, which was originally borrowed from the game of baccarat, is an elongated plastic box into which pre-shuffled cards are stacked. One end of the box has a slot and a finger notch so that the dealer may easily slide out the cards, one at a time.

The Shuffling Machine
To speed up the game, many blackjack tables are now equipped with an automatic shuffling machine or a continuous shuffling machine.

The Cards
The game of blackjack uses one or more standard 52-card decks with the jokers removed. Each deck consists of thirteen cards in each of four suits: spades, hearts, clubs, and diamonds.

Card Values
In blackjack, the value of a hand is purely numeric; the card suits have no meaning and are completely disre-

garded. Only the numeric values of the cards are relevant. The numeric value of the cards 2 through 10 are counted as their face value. That is, a 5 of spades counts as 5, and a 9 of hearts counts as 9.

The face cards, jack, queen, and king, are valued the same as a 10 card. Any reference to ten-value or ten-count cards always includes the jack, queen, and king, as well as the 10 spot. Any statement that a hand contains a 10 means that it contains one of the ten-value cards. In a 52-card deck there are sixteen ten-value cards. Thus, over 30% or better of the cards in each deck have a value of 10.

In blackjack, the ace possesses the unusual trait of having a dual numeric value. It can be a one-count card or an eleven-count card, and automatically takes on the value that is most beneficial to the hand. Clearly, the ace is a very significant card in blackjack. Since an ace is needed to complete a natural, it is also a very important card for the player.

Chips

The standard casino chips used in other games may also be played at a blackjack table. They should be chips issued by the casino in which you are playing—chips from another casino may not be accepted. Currency may also be wagered at a blackjack table, but winnings are always paid in casino chips.

The exception to this is roulette chips, which cannot be used at any other game, even in the same casino. These special non-value chips should never be taken away from the roulette table where they were issued, but must always be turned in to the roulette dealer in exchange for regular casino chips.

THE PLAYERS' HANDS

Now that you understand the equipment, we'll take a look at the terminology for the different kinds of hands you can get. When a multiple deck shoe is used, the players' cards are always dealt face up. Since the playing rules for the dealer are fixed, in an honest game with an honest dealer, it doesn't matter if the player's hand is dealt face up or face down. In either case, a player's initial hand consists of two cards, which may be categorized in the following ways.

Hard Hand

This is an initial hand that does not contain an ace and has a total count of more than 11. It is called *hard* because the total numeric value of the hand is fixed and an additional card can cause it to exceed a count of 21. For instance, if the two dealt cards are a 5 and a 9, the hand has a hard value of 14. A third card of 8 or higher will result in a total greater than 21.

Soft Hand

This is an initial hand in which one of the cards is an ace. It is called *soft* because the ace can have a numeric value of 11 without the total going over 21. Although, a hand consisting of a 4 and an ace may have a total value of either 5 or 15, it is called a soft 15. The main feature of a soft total is that it cannot be busted (as will be discussed in greater detail), since the value of the ace can always be changed to 1. However, once the ace has to be changed to a 1 to prevent busting, it becomes a hard hand.

In the above example, any additional cards that add up to more than 6 points convert the soft 15 to a hard hand because the ace would have to be a 1 to keep the total from exceeding 21. For instance, if the third card is an 8, the hand becomes a hard 13 (A, 4, 8). Whenever the value of the ace has to be changed from 11 to 1 to prevent busting, it becomes a hard hand.

Thus, an initial hand with two aces is a special case. Although it may have a value of 2 or 12, this is almost immaterial because in actual play the best strategy is to always split the aces into two separate hands.

Pat and Stiff Hands

A **pat hand** is one that cannot reasonably be improved. In blackjack, any hand with a hard count of 17 through 21 is considered pat. A **stiff hand** is one that is not pat and can be busted with the addition of a single card. Specifically, any hand with a hard total of 12 through 16 is considered stiff.

Blackjack (Natural)

A **blackjack** is a two-card hand consisting of an ace plus any ten-count card dealt on the first two cards only. Another name for a blackjack hand is a **natural**. In this book I will use the term *natural* to avoid confusion with the name of the game.

A natural is the best hand a player can get on the initial deal, and is an automatic winner if the dealer doesn't also have a natural. A winning natural pays 3 to 2, that is, a $10 bet will win $15, and a $25 bet will win $37.50. The payoff should always be exactly 3 to 2, right down to the small change.

Since all other winning bets and hands in blackjack are paid even money, a natural is very good for the player. If the dealer also has a natural, however, the player's hand is tied and no money is won or lost. This is called a **push**. On average, a player will be dealt one natural about every 21 hands.

Occasionally, the payoff for a natural will be something other than 3 to 2. In the past, some casinos have held promotions for limited periods during which naturals were paid at 8 to 5 or even 2 to 1. Recently, some Las Vegas Strip casinos have offered single-deck games with only a 6 to 5 payoff for naturals. They claim that their playing rules are so enhanced that they have to shortchange the natural payoffs to balance the game. In fact, the rules are no better than in many other casinos that pay the standard 3 to 2.

It is unlikely, however, that you will encounter a multiple deck game that pays less than 3 to 2 for a natural. If you do, make sure all your friends know about it so they can avoid that casino.

Busted Hand
When, in the course of drawing additional cards, the total point count of the hand goes over 21, it is said to be **busted**. When that happens, the hand is an immediate loser; the dealer collects the bet and places the player's cards in the discard tray. The dealer's hand can be busted

as well; however, since the dealer plays last, if the dealer busts, the busted player still loses.

PLAYER OPTIONS

Now that you've examined your initial two cards and determined if they are hard, soft, stiff, or pat, what can you do with them? A number of different player options are available, all of which are reviewed below. Some actions are communicated to the dealer with hand signals, while others are communicated by simply increasing the initial wager.

Hit

If you are not satisfied with the two-card count, you may request additional cards, one by one. This is called taking a **hit**. Indicate your desire to take a hit by pointing at your cards with an index finger. Some players prefer to tap or scratch the felt directly behind the cards. Either way is acceptable. You may hit as many times as you want, so long as you don't go over 21. If the card count exceeds 21, you have busted and your bet is lost. If you bust, the dealer will immediately remove your bet and your cards from the layout.

Stand

When you are satisfied with the card count and don't want any more hits, you may **stand**. Signal your intention to stand by waving your hand over the cards, palm down. You can stand at any time: after looking at your original hand, after taking one or more hits, or after splitting a pair. Standing is automatic if you double down (see below) because you are given just one card and are not allowed to take any hits.

Double Down

You may double down on certain hands by placing another wager in the same amount as your original bet. Some casinos permit you to bet less than the amount of your original wager. Indicate your desire to double down by placing the new wager alongside your original bet.

You will then receive one additional card from the dealer and will not be permitted to take any further action on that hand. This is good strategy when your hand reaches a total of 10 or 11 and the dealer is showing a low card. Because of the prevalence of ten-value cards in the deck, you are hoping to get a 20 or 21.

The rules for doubling vary. Some casinos allow doubling only on the first two cards dealt; others allow doubling after splitting a pair. Some casinos permit doubling on any two-card count; others restrict doubling to a total count of 10 or 11. The dealer will tell you whether or not you can double on a particular hand.

Split

Whenever you are dealt a pair, that is, two cards of equal rank, you have the option of splitting those cards into two separate hands. At almost all casinos, you may split any ten-value cards; that is, you could split a hand consisting of a jack and a king. However, splitting ten-value cards is not a recommended strategy and you should never do it.

Indicate your desire to split by placing a second wager alongside your original bet. It must be for the same amount as the original bet. Before acting on your signal, the dealer may ask if you intend to double or split.

With a pair of fives, for instance, most dealers know that splitting is not good strategy, but doubling may be appropriate.

When it is clear that you are splitting, the dealer gives you two more cards, one on each of your original cards, so that you are now playing two hands of two cards each. You should then continue playing as if they are initial hands. The dealer will point to the first hand and wait for your signal. When you stand on that hand, she will point to the other one. You may play these hands the same as any other, except that some casinos do not permit doubling down or any further splitting.

A pair of aces is a special case. If you split aces (which is always recommended), you will be given one card on each ace and will not be allowed to take a hit or take any further action.

Resplit

If, when you split a pair, one or both of the cards you get from the dealer are the same rank as the original pair, you may split again. This is called **resplitting**. For instance, if you split a pair of eights and received another eight, you could resplit into three hands. Some casinos do not allow resplitting.

Again, aces are a special case. Most casinos that permit resplitting do not permit aces to be resplit.

Surrender

If you don't like what you see when you are dealt the first two cards, you may **surrender** (fold) your hand and forfeit half of your bet. If you decide to surrender, simply say that you are surrendering, and the dealer will take half of your bet and toss your cards into the discard tray. Once you take the first hit, you lose this option. You also lose it if the dealer has a natural, in which case you lose your entire bet. In a few specific instances, surrender is a useful option.

The above form of surrender is sometimes referred to as *late surrender* to distinguish it from *early surrender*. In early surrender, you still only lose half your bet if the dealer has a natural, which is much more favorable for the player. Early surrender was offered in Atlantic City when the first casinos opened there, but it didn't last very long. Smart players and card counters took advantage of it and the casinos managed to get the rules changed. Today, the early surrender option is almost nonexistent, so when I talk about surrender in this book I always mean late surrender.

Insurance

If the dealer's upcard is an ace, the dealer will call out, "Insurance," and you are offered the opportunity to place an insurance side bet. You do this by putting up to half the amount of your original bet on the layout area marked: *Insurance pays 2 to 1*. If, after peeking at her hole card, the dealer turns up a natural, any insurance bets are paid off at 2 to 1. If the dealer does not have a natural, the insurance side bet is lost. For a basic strategy player, this is not a good wager. Don't ever do it.

If you have a natural showing and the dealer's upcard is an Ace, the dealer may ask, "Even money?" This is the same as the insurance bet because if the dealer also has a natural, you will push on the natural and get paid 2 to 1 on your insurance bet. If the dealer does not have a natural, you will win 3 to 2 on your natural and lose the insurance bet. In either case, the result is an even money payout. Be sure to decline the even money offer because most of the time, you will win at 3 to 2.

DEALER FUNCTIONS

As a representative of the casino, the dealer manages and controls the blackjack game. She converts a player's money into chips, deals out the cards, collects chips from the losers, and pays the winners. She also enforces the table betting limits and makes sure that all players follow the table rules.

Converting Cash into Chips

You can place bets using either money or casino chips. If you need to convert a bill to chips, place it next to or above the betting box—never hand it to the dealer. Be careful not to place it in a betting box (unless you intend to bet) for the dealer might think it is a bet and deal out a hand.

The dealer will not stop to convert your cash until the current hand is concluded, so don't think she is ignoring you. If you lay out a large bill, it will be entirely converted to chips; the dealer cannot make change. You may, however, ask for specific denominations of chips. The common terms for $5 chips are **nickels** or **reds**; for $25 chips, they are **quarters** or **greens**. The denomination is always indicated on the center of the chip, along with the name of the casino.

When you quit playing and are ready to change your chips back to cash, you have to do that at the cashier's cage. The cashier's cage is also the only place where you can cash traveler's checks, money orders, or personal checks. If you present one of these items to the dealer, she will direct you to the cashier.

To make payoffs easier and faster, the dealer will often pay winners with high-denomination chips. If you have accumulated a stack of greens, but would prefer to play reds, just ask the dealer for change. If you leave the table with a big pile of chips, you can ask the dealer to convert them to a larger denomination so that they are easier to handle. This is called **changing color**.

Shuffling

Most multiple deck games use either four, six, or eight decks of cards, all shuffled together. Assuming a continuous shuffling machine (CSM) is not used, the dealer will manually shuffle all the decks together. Shuffling six or eight decks is a tedious and slow procedure, so many casinos now use automatic shuffling machines (which are different than CSMs). After shuffling, the dealer will square up the 6- or 8-deck pack, set it down sideways and hand one of the players a colored cut card.

The player is supposed to slide the card into the pack. If you are offered the cut and decline it (which is your option), the dealer will offer it to the next player.

The dealer will break the pack at the colored card and make the cut. She will then reinsert the cut card in the pack, one to four decks from the back end, depending on the policy of the casino, and place the pack into the dealing shoe. The cut card is now an indicator to the dealer as to when she has to reshuffle. Finally, she will draw the first card from the shoe and place it into the discard tray. This is called the **burn card**. Burning a card is an old anti-cheating measure in case someone has seen the top card of the pack.

When a CSM is used, most of the above shuffling procedure is eliminated. The machine, which is combined with a dealing shoe, shuffles four or five decks of cards continuously and feeds them to the dealer one at a time. The dealer periodically places discards into the machine, which get randomly mixed with the unplayed cards.

Since the machine continuously shuffles the cards, the dealer never has to interrupt the game to shuffle. More and more casinos are installing CSMs because they speed up play by about 20% and, thereby, increase the table income by the same amount. They also completely thwart card counting.

Dealing

The cards are dealt out in a clockwise direction, starting from the dealer's left. Every player who has put out a bet is dealt two cards, usually face up. Whenever the player's cards are dealt face up, the player can look, but can't touch—all the card handling is done by the dealer. The dealer also gets two cards, one face up called the **upcard** and one face down called the **downcard** or the

hole card. Later on, we'll describe an unconventional variation called **Double Exposure**, in which both of the dealer's cards are dealt face up.

Checking for a Natural

If the dealer's upcard is an ace or any ten-value card, she peeks at her downcard to see if she has a natural. If she does, the hand is terminated and everyone loses automatically, except those players who also have naturals. Remember, when the dealer and a player both have naturals, it is considered a push and no money changes hands.

Since a dealer's natural is settled at the beginning of a round, the players never have an opportunity to increase their bets by doubling or splitting. Consequently, any player who doesn't also have a natural only loses his initial wager.

Advance knowledge of the dealer's downcard is of great benefit to a player, so when the dealer peeks, there is always the danger of cheating. A dishonest dealer may signal the value of the hole card to a confederate at the table, or a player may get a glimpse of it. To prevent these things from happening, some casinos have changed the peeking rules. Sometimes the dealer may only peek if the upcard is an ace, and sometimes she isn't supposed to peek at all.

When the dealer doesn't peek or only peeks under aces, a dealer's natural may not be apparent until everyone has finished playing out his hand. What about those players who increased their bets by doubling or splitting? In the

United States, the extra bets are ignored and the players only lose their initial wagers.

In some parts of the world, mainly in Europe, the dealer's hole card is not even dealt out until all the players have acted on their hands. In this case, all players' bets made as a result of doubling and splitting are lost to a dealer's natural. This is referred to as the **European no-hole-card rule**. In the United States, you may occasionally run into a greedy casino that applies the no-hole-card rule, but this has never occurred in Nevada or New Jersey—not yet, anyway.

Dealer's Playing Rules

After all the players have acted on their hands, the dealer turns over her hole card for all to see and either stands or hits her hand. She can not double down or split—those are options reserved for the players. Assuming she doesn't have a natural, the dealer has to play her hand according to a fixed casino rule. In most casinos that rule is: Dealer must draw on all totals of 16 or less, and stand on all totals of 17 or more. The rule is always imprinted on the felt tabletop, and is usually stated as: *Dealer must draw to 16 and stand on all 17s.*

This rule is standard in most venues, including Atlantic City and Europe. However, many casinos have modified the rule so that their dealers have to take a hit if they have a soft total of exactly 17. In that case, the rule imprinted on the felt is stated as: *Dealer must hit soft 17s.*

It is understood that the dealer must draw to 16 and stand on hard 17.

When the dealer hits soft 17s, it is less favorable for the player and increases the casino's edge by 0.2 %. This rule is mainly applied in downtown Las Vegas, some casinos on the Strip, and some casinos in Mississippi. At least it is easy to tell what rule applies by glancing at the tabletop, which is more than can be said for rarely posted rule variations on player doubling and splitting.

Payoffs

When the dealer has finished playing her hand, she compares it to all players' hands that haven't busted. As you've learned, any player who has a natural is an automatic winner if the dealer doesn't also have a natural, and is paid off at 3 to 2. If the dealer peeked at her hole card at the start of the round, the naturals will already have been paid. If the dealer also has a natural, it is a push and no money is exchanged.

Of the rest of the players, those with a higher total than the dealer are paid even money; that is, the dealer will pay them an amount equal to their total wager. Players with a total count less than the dealer lose their bets. Any hand with a point total equal to the dealer's is a push.

A NOTE ON PAYOFFS

A payoff described as *even money* is the same as a payoff of 1 to 1. In other words, if you wager $10 and win, you will be paid an additional $10. If you get a natural, you will be paid off at 3 to 2. In other words, you will be paid three dollars for every two dollars that you bet, and you get to keep your original two dollar bet.

For instance, if you had a $10 bet out (say, two $5 chips) and were dealt a natural, the dealer will leave your bet in place and give you another $15 (three $5 chips). In those games where a natural pays 6 to 5, your $10 bet would only win $12.

Occasionally, you may see payoff odds stated as 2 *for* 1 instead of 2 *to* 1. On a 2 to 1 payoff, if you wager $10 and win, you will be paid $20 *and* get to keep your original bet. If the payoff is stated as 2 *for* 1, you will also be paid $20, but will lose your original $10, so that your net win is only $20. Thus, odds of 2 *for* 1 is the same as an even money bet. This is a little deception that doesn't fool professionals, but can easily mislead the casual gambler.

SUMMARY OF BLACKJACK FUNDAMENTALS

PLAYER HANDS

HARD HAND — Does not contain an ace and has a total count of 12 or more.

SOFT HAND — Contains an ace that can be valued at 11 without busting in the hand.

PAT HAND — A hard total of 17 through 21.

STIFF HAND — A hard total of 12 through 16.

NATURAL — An initial hand consisting of an ace and any ten-count card. Also called blackjack.

PLAYER OPTIONS

HIT — A request for an additional card.

STAND — A decision to not take further action.

DOUBLE DOWN — Taking a hit of only one card in return for doubling the original bet.

SPLIT — Converting a pair into two separate hands, with the same bet on each hand.

RESPLIT — Splitting an additional time after getting another card of the same rank.

SURRENDER — Folding the initial hand in return for giving up half of the original bet.

INSURANCE — A 2 to 1 side bet on whether or not the dealer has a natural.

3

BLACKJACK RULE VARIATIONS

When the only legal casinos in the United States were located in Nevada and New Jersey, the rules of casino blackjack were fairly well standardized. At that time, there were only a few minor rule variances between the two states. There were also some minor differences between the main venues in Nevada, namely the Las Vegas Strip, downtown Las Vegas, and Northern Nevada.

Today, much of that has changed. With the proliferation of legal casinos in Mississippi, Louisiana, Illinois, and other states, along with the expansion of tribal casinos throughout the country, blackjack playing rules can no longer be easily defined by venue. The one exception is Atlantic City, where the rules are controlled by statute rather than by the individual casinos. In the following sections, I will describe the various rules and try to organize them in an understandable way.

STANDARD RULES
Before getting into the rule variations, it would be useful to establish a set of *standard rules* as a baseline. The problem is that there is no single set of blackjack rules used by the majority of casinos. In fact, within some casinos the rules can change from one table to the next.

The only uniform venue in the United States is Atlantic City. Since the multiple deck rules used in Atlantic City are reasonably good for the player, I will use them in this book as our standard baseline.

STANDARD BASELINE BLACKJACK RULES
(ATLANTIC CITY)

1. Six- or eight-deck game.
2. Dealer must stand on all 17s.
3. Resplitting of pairs allowed (except aces).
4. Double down on any two cards.
5. Double down after splitting allowed.
6. Surrender is not an option.
7. All ties are pushes.
8. Natural pays 3 to 2.
9. Lose all to a dealer natural.

Six- or Eight-Deck Game

The multiple deck game is an important part of our standard baseline rules because it is the primary aim of this book. Six- or eight-deck games are found in every legal casino in the world, and in Atlantic City they are the only games available. The sole disadvantage of a multi-deck game is that it increases the house edge by up to 0.57% more than a single-deck game.

If you see a continuous shuffling machine (CSM), consider it the same as a multiple deck game. CSMs have been disparaged by blackjack players, believing that casinos would not have made the investment if they didn't derive some benefit—probably to the detriment of the players. The only detriment is to card counters, who are probably the biggest complainers. With a CSM, each new hand is effectively dealt from a freshly shuffled deck, making it impossible to maintain a count.

There is also a financial benefit to the casinos. Since the delay caused by shuffling and loading the shoe has been eliminated, about 20% more hands can be dealt every hour. Consequently, the net return from a table is increased by the same percentage.

For a non-counting basic strategy player (such as you), playing at a CSM-equipped table has no disadvantage. In fact, computer simulations have proved that a CSM reduces the house edge by 0.02% when compared to a hand-shuffled six-deck game.

The mathematical reason for this gets a little complicated and has to do with something called the **cut card effect**. The insertion of a cut card (designed to make counting more difficult) instead of dealing out all the decks is also slightly detrimental to the non-counting player. Since there is no cut card in a CSM-dealt game, the house loses this mathematical advantage. (You may be glad to know that I won't go into the technical explanation of the cut card effect.)

Dealer Must Stand on All 17s

As described in the last chapter, this is the rule where the dealer must draw on all totals of 16 or less, and stand on all totals of 17 or more. It is easy to determine which games apply this rule because it is always imprinted on the felt tabletop. In Atlantic City, this rule is required.

Resplitting of Pairs Allowed

When you split a pair and one or both of the cards you get from the dealer are the same rank as the original pair, you may split again. Since most casinos do not allow resplitting of aces, you will have to ask the dealer or a floor supervisor if resplitting is allowed at any particular table.

Double Down on Any Two Cards

This rule has to be specified in our baseline because some casinos only allow doubling on certain totals. You will have to ask the dealer about any doubling restrictions.

Double Down After Splitting Allowed

After splitting a pair into two hands, some casinos allow you to double down on one or both of the hands. This is a standard rule in Atlantic City. Elsewhere you will have to ask the dealer or a floor supervisor if doubling after splitting is permitted.

Surrender Not an Option

In some casinos, you may fold (surrender) your hand and forfeit half of your bet if you don't like your first two cards. Since it is not an option in Atlantic City, it is also not an option in our baseline.

All Ties are Pushes

If your hand ties the dealer's, you neither win nor lose and no money changes hands. This is a standard rule in casino blackjack, so you don't need to ask about it. If, on occasion, a casino gets greedy and changes this rule, you will know about it quickly enough.

Natural Pays 3 to 2

Assuming the dealer also doesn't have a natural (which would be a push), your natural will pay off at 3 to 2. This is often (but not always) imprinted on the felt. In any case, the rule is so standard that you don't need to ask. When a casino changes this rule, they almost always place a sign to that effect on the table.

COMMON RULE VARIATIONS

The rule variations described in this section are found in most gambling jurisdictions. Most of the variations are minor and have only a small effect on the house edge.

Common Rule Variations

1. Single-, double-, or four-deck game.
2. Dealer must hit soft 17.
3. Double down restrictions.
4. No double down after splitting.
5. Lose all to a natural.
6. Resplitting aces allowed.
7. Surrender is an option.

Single-, Double-, or Four-Deck Game

One, two, or four-deck games are not as prevalent as six or eight-deck games because they give the player a better advantage. However, in most cases, other rules are changed to compensate for this and bring the house edge back up again. A few one or two-deck games can be found in most gambling venues in the United States, except Atlantic City.

Dealer Must Hit Soft 17

When the dealer hits a soft 17, the rule is always imprinted on the felt tabletop. This rule, which increases the house edge by 0.2%, used to be found only in Northern Nevada and downtown Las Vegas. Now it has spread to many Strip casinos, riverboat casinos, and tribal casinos. Atlantic City casinos still stand on a soft 17.

Double Down Restrictions

Most casinos allow doubling down on any two-card total, but some casinos impose limitations. In Northern Nevada and downtown Las Vegas (except the Golden Nugget), for instance, you may double down only on a total of 10 or 11, giving the casino an added advantage of about 0.2%. In Europe, doubling is restricted to 9, 10, or 11, which increases the house edge by 0.1%.

No Doubling Down After Splitting

Many casinos do not allow you to double down after splitting, which increases the house edge by more than 0.1%. You will have to ask the dealer or a floor supervisor if doubling after splitting is permitted.

Lose All to a Natural

In some casinos, where the dealer does not peek at the hole card, or it is not dealt until all the players have acted on their hands, all increased bets made as a result of doubling and splitting are lost to a dealer's natural.

Resplitting Aces Allowed

After splitting a pair of aces, some casinos permit resplitting a third ace. This is a minor benefit to the player, amounting to less than a 0.1% gain.

BLACKJACK RULE VARIATIONS

Surrender is an Option

If you don't like your initial hand, some casinos allow you to fold your hand in return for half of your bet. This is a minor benefit to the player—less than 0.1%. When surrender is offered, it is almost always at a multiple deck game. It is no longer an option in Atlantic City, but can be found at most Strip casinos as well as many riverboat and tribal casinos.

UNUSUAL RULE VARIATIONS

This section covers less common rule variations that are occasionally used for promotions or in special versions of blackjack. They are listed mainly so that you can avoid such games when the rules are applied inappropriately by greedy casinos.

Unusual Rule Variations
1. Six-card automatic winner.
2. Resplitting of pairs not allowed.
3. Natural payoff better than 3 to 2.
4. Natural payoff worse than 3 to 2.
5. Dealer wins all ties.

Six-Card Automatic Winner

Every so often a casino may consider a six-card unbusted hand an automatic winner, which improves the player's edge by 0.15%. Although this rule is common in some unconventional blackjack games, in standard blackjack it is usually part of a promotion.

Resplitting of Pairs Not Allowed

ALthough this is rare, you may run into a casino that does not permit resplitting of any pair. This raises the casino edge by less than 0.1%.

Natural Payoff
Better than 3 to 2

Every so often a casino runs a limited-time promotion in which naturals are paid at 8 to 5 or even 2 to 1. Such promotions are very short term because a 2 to 1 payoff improves the player's edge by over 2%.

Natural Payoff
Worse than 3 to 2

Much more often you will find reduced payoffs of 6 to 5 or even 1 to 1. The 1 to 1 payoff is found in a copyrighted single-deck version called "Super Fun 21." Some casinos have gotten around the copyright by offering a similar game with a 6 to 5 payoff on naturals. A reduced payoff for a natural is almost always indicated by a sign on the table. The good news is that reduced payoffs are not likely to be found in multiple deck games.

Dealer Wins all Ties

This mainly occurs in private home games and in a modified casino game called "Double Exposure," in which both dealer's cards are dealt face up. These games are covered later in this book.

4

ANALYZING THE GAME

Now that we know how to play blackjack, we need to learn how to play it well. Before getting into the actual playing strategies, however, it would be very helpful to develop a deeper understanding of the game. In addition to outlining the player's rights and the casino's advantage, this chapter contains evaluations of all the dealer upcards and player hands.

PLAYER RIGHTS

A blackjack player has rights? You bet! You have the right to wager any amount of money within the minimum and maximum table limits. After receiving your first two cards, you have the right to split any pair into two hands, which effectively doubles your bet. Of course, you only want to double your bet if it is beneficial, and the basic strategy in the following chapters will tell you when to do that.

You may also double your wager by doubling down on your first two cards, if it appears to be advantageous. Some casinos permit you to also double down after splitting. Consequently, under some circumstances, you can end up betting four times as much as your original wager (by splitting, and doubling on each split hand) if you think you have good enough cards. If you resplit, your total wager can get even higher.

Splitting and doubling down are benefits that allow you to increase your wager if you think you have potentially-winning cards. These advantages are all yours because the dealer can't split or double down under any circumstances. Since ties are pushes and the dealer has to actually beat your hand to win, you might think these player benefits are enough to win consistently. However, we know that the casino wouldn't even be offering the game unless it was sure of winning in the long run. The truth is that the house has one major advantage that overcomes all the benefits given to the players. That advantage is the fact that the dealer plays her hand last.

THE CASINO'S ADVANTAGE
Playing out your hand before the dealer plays hers gives the casino a major advantage that is difficult to overcome. If, when you play your hand, you end up busting, you have automatically lost no matter what happens to the dealer's hand. For a more dramatic illustration, assume that all the players at a full blackjack table manage to bust their hands. If the dealer also busts, the house still wins all the wagers on the table.

There are two ways to diminish this major edge held by the house. The first is to play your hand correctly by exactly following the basic strategy rules. Doing this can reduce the house edge to where it approaches an even game.

The second is to track (count) cards in addition to applying the basic strategy. Doing this can reduce the house edge to zero and even swing it in favor of the player. Card counting, however, is not covered in this book. It is a specialized technique that requires a high level of study, practice, and concentration. When you become an expert basic strategy player and want to try your hand at counting, there are at least a dozen excellent books available on the subject (and two dozen poor ones).

So, what is the house edge when you play your hand exactly according to the basic strategy? That depends on several factors, including the number of decks used and the particular playing rules in use at a given table. This book concentrates on multiple deck games, so the house edge is mainly dependent on the specific house rules that are in effect.

The best of the commonly-found set of rules for multiple deck games or games using a continuous shuffling machine (CSM) are the Standard Blackjack Rules that I established as a baseline in the previous chapter. Depending on the number of decks used, these rules give the house an edge of 0.39% to 0.43%, as shown in the following table:

STANDARD BASELINE RULES

Decks Used	House Edge
Eight	0.43%
Six	0.41%
CSM	0.39%

In this chapter, I use the convention that a positive percentage favors the house, and a negative percentage favors the player (because it reduces the house edge). As you can see in the table, the multiple deck house edge is well under one-half of one percent, so it is still pretty good for the player. Especially when compared to a game such as roulette with a 5.26% house edge. Other rules can make the standard baseline number a little better or a little worse, as shown in the following list.

PERCENT CHANGES FOR RULE VARIATIONS

Resplitting aces allowed	-0.05%
Surrender option	-0.05%
Aces can be resplit	-0.08%
Six-card automatic winner	-0.15%
One deck (instead of 8 decks)	-0.57%
One deck (instead of 6 decks)	-0.55%
Two decks (instead of 8 decks)	-0.24%
Two decks (instead of 6 decks)	-0.21%
Pair resplitting not allowed	+0.10%
No double after splitting	+0.14%
Dealer must hit soft 17	+0.22%
Double on 9, 10, or 11 only	+0.10%
Double on 10 or 11 only	+0.18%
Lose all to a natural	+0.10%
Natural payoff 6 to 5	+1.40%
Natural payoff 1 to 1	+2.30%
Dealer wins all ties	+8.85%

The above percentages assume that you are using perfect basic strategy. Basic strategy is the heart of this book and will be covered quite thoroughly in the following chapters. Applying it is not as difficult as it sounds, and after enough practice, it should become second nature.

ANALYZING THE GAME

Working with the numbers in the chart is easier than it looks. Let's say you go to downtown Las Vegas and find a six-deck table where the dealer must hit soft 17, and they only permit you to double on 10 or 11. To calculate this, start with +0.41% for the six-deck game, add +0.22% for hitting soft 17, and add +0.18% for restricted doubling, as shown below.

Six-deck game	+0.41%
Dealer must hit soft 17	+0.22%
Double on 10 or 11 only	+0.18%
Net casino edge =	+0.81%

Even with limited doubling and with the dealer hitting soft 17, the casino edge is less than 1%.

For a slightly more complicated example, you find a CSM game on the Strip with standard rules except that surrender is allowed and doubling after splitting is not allowed. Simply start with +0.39% for CSM and reduce it by -0.05% for surrender and increase it by +0.14% for no doubling, as shown below.

CSM game	+0.39%
Surrender allowed	-0.05%
No double after splitting	+0.14%
Net casino edge =	+0.48%

You can't do much better than a multi-deck or CSM game with a house edge of less than half of one percent.

THE DEALER'S UPCARD

Since the dealer's hole card remains a mystery until she plays her hand, the dealer's upcard is the only additional clue you have for deciding how to play your hand. This is a very important clue that should never be ignored. In fact, the entire playing strategy for blackjack, that you will be learning in the next chapter, is strongly dependent on the value of this card.

Dealer's Ace

This is the most dangerous card for the player. With an ace up, the dealer has about a 30% chance of having a natural. It also gives the dealer the lowest chance of busting—12% to 14%, depending on whether or not she has to hit a soft 17. If the dealer does not have a natural, however, a player who reaches a count of 19, 20, or 21, has a good chance of beating the dealer.

Dealer's 10

A 10 is also a very strong upcard for the dealer, with a 79% chance of standing on a 17 or better, and a 34% chance of getting a 20. Even when the dealer doesn't have a natural, with a hole card of 7 or higher, she will have a pat hand. If you don't hit your hard hand of 16 or less, you will lose more than three out of four times.

Dealer's 9

With this card, the dealer will end up with a count of 19 more than 35% of the time. Yes, she will bust 23% of the time, but that means if you don't have a pat hand you will lose 77% of the time. Whatever you do, don't stand on that 15 or 16!

Dealer's 8

For the player, this is almost like the 9, except that it is one point lower and slightly easier to beat. The dealer will most likely be standing on 18. If you don't have an 18 or better, you will lose more than half of the time.

Dealer's 7

With a 7, the dealer will stand on 17 almost 37% of the time, and bust 26% of the time. Now things are looking up. A 17 isn't that hard to beat, but you had better hit that 12-16 or you will still lose three out of four times.

Dealer's 4, 5, or 6

These are the happy dealer upcards. When a 4, 5, or 6 shows, you can look around the table and see the smiles. The dealer's chance of busting has suddenly become 40% to 44%. Now you can stand on your stiff hand and come out ahead on the deal.

Dealer's 2 or 3

These upcards are almost as happy as 4, 5, or 6, even though the dealer has a smaller chance of busting (35% to 37%). The basic strategy rules are different than for the 4, 5, or 6 upcards, so pay attention when you get to that chapter.

THE PLAYER'S HAND
Count of 21

Whoopie! With two cards, you have a natural and get paid 3 to 2 (if the dealer doesn't also have a natural). With three or more cards, you have the dealer beat 88% to 96% of the time, depending on the upcard—and the rest of the time you will push.

Count of 20

This should make you happy, too. It's not as good as a 21, but it is a strong winning hand. You will learn in the basic strategy chapters never to ruin a solid 20 by splitting a pair of 10s.

Count of 19

Not as good as a 20, but good enough to win most of the time. Since this is already a winning hand, you should always stand, even if it is soft.

Count of 18

This is a marginal hand which will win (or lose) about 50% of the time. If it is a hard 18, such as an 8-10, it is far too risky to hit. If it is an ace-7 (or some other soft combination, such as an ace-5-2), you should try to improve it if the dealer shows a 9, 10, or ace. If your 18 consists of a pair of 9s, you should strictly follow the splitting rules in the basic strategy.

Count of 17

A hard 17, such as an 8-9, is one of the worst hands you can have. It is too risky to hit because any card higher than a 4 will bust the hand. If the dealer doesn't bust, the best you can do is push. An ace-6 however, is much better. In fact, you should hit (or double if appropriate) any soft 17 regardless of the dealer's upcard.

Hard 12-16

These hands have the highest risk of busting, but when the dealer is showing a 7 or higher, you have to hit to limit your losses. For dealer upcards of 2 through 6, standing and hoping the dealer will bust is your best strategy. The exception is when you have a 12 and the dealer shows a 2 or 3. In that case, hitting is slightly better.

When you have a 16 consisting of a pair of 8s, you should always split. This action converts one terrible hand into two that are much better.

Count of 11 or Less

sSince these hands cannot be busted, some action (such as hitting, doubling, or splitting) should always be taken to improve the total. The basic strategy in the following chapters will tell you precisely what to do.

Pairs

The basic strategy will also tell you how to handle pairs. An ace-ace, for example, should always be split. I mention that here because it is an important rule to remember. Previously I admonished you against splitting ten-value cards. For the same reason, you should never split a pair of 5s; why ruin a good hand to end up with two poor ones? What you do with most other pairs depends on the dealer's upcard.

5

STRATEGIES FOR THE NOVICE

Before employing the various playing strategies for blackjack, it is important that you first become familiar with the proper decision-making procedure. Knowledge of the playing strategies will be of limited value if you try to apply them haphazardly. There is a certain evaluation sequence that should be followed in order to make the best playing decisions.

PLAYING DECISIONS

Many novice blackjack players get flustered when it is their turn to make a decision on how to play their hand. Should they split? Should they double down? Should they hit? Should they stand? Suddenly there seem to be an unending number of decisions to make. Although they have carefully memorized the strategy rules, when their turn comes and the dealer is impatiently pointing at their hand, they draw a blank and end up taking the wrong action.

Experienced players, on the other hand, don't have a problem when it comes time to make a decision because they already use such a methodical approach on a subconscious level. It is so automatic that most of them don't even realize they are doing it. Whether subconscious or not, if you follow the decision process outlined below while applying the basic strategy, you have the best chance of playing your hand correctly.

Decide...
Whether or Not to Surrender
Apply the basic strategy rules to determine if surrendering is the best action. If surrendering is not an option or you are using one of the simplified strategy tables, skip to pair splitting.

Decide...
Whether or Not to Split a Pair
Apply the basic strategy rules to determine if splitting is the best action. If your initial hand is not a pair, skip to doubling.

Decide...
Whether or Not to Double Down
Whether or not you have split a pair, apply the basic strategy rules to determine if doubling is the next best action.

Decide...
Whether to Hit or Stand
If you did not double, apply the basic strategy rules to determine if you should hit or stand.

If you split a pair, repeat the above steps for each hand. These four fundamental playing decisions are summarized in the following simple, easy-to-remember chart:

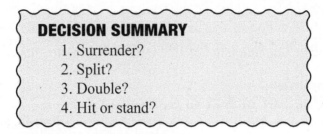

DECISION SUMMARY
1. Surrender?
2. Split?
3. Double?
4. Hit or stand?

THE NOVICE STRATEGIES

When you are a beginner, learning the entire Universal Basic Strategy table (see the next chapter), seems like a daunting task—especially when you are anxious to start playing. As an aid to novices, I have broken the task down to three parts. First you learn the Really Simple Strategy. Then, as you gain a little experience, you learn the Abridged Basic Strategy. Finally, you will find it relatively easy to expand your knowledge by learning the full Universal Basic Strategy table, one section at a time.

For all these strategies assume Standard Blackjack Rules as used in Atlantic City where doubling after splitting is allowed.

A REALLY SIMPLE STRATEGY

This is as simple as it gets. Surprisingly, using the **Really Simple Strategy** costs the player less than one percent as compared to the Abridged Basic Strategy shown later in this chapter. That is, the total house advantage will still be less than 2%—which is a whole lot better than the 3% to 5% advantage the house has over the average player.

The main differences between this strategy and the full-blown basic strategy are the lack of a surrender option and greatly-simplified splitting and doubling rules. Also, soft hands are treated the same as hard hands. Before you ever step up to a blackjack table, be sure you have the following rules down pat, and have familiarized yourself with the decision-making procedure in this section. If you don't, you might as well just hand your wallet to the pit boss.

Pair of Aces

Always split a pair of aces. The value of the initial hand is either a 2 or a soft 12, neither of which is very good. By splitting, you get two chances of catching 21s. Remember, an ace-10 on a split is only a 21, not a natural. Remember also that splitting aces is a special case. The dealer will give you just one card on each ace, and you cannot take any hits. If one of those cards is another ace, you should resplit to a third hand, if the casino permits you to do so.

Pair of 8s

Always split a pair of 8s. The value of the initial hand is 16, which is the worst hand you can have. Splitting the eights limits your losses. The dealer will give you one card on each 8, and if one of those cards is another 8, you should resplit to a third hand. Now you can commence playing the hands, one at a time, according to the rules below.

Any Other Pair

Some of the remaining pairs should never be split and others should only be split when the dealer shows certain cards. This is where the rules get more complicated, so to play it safe in the Really Simple Strategy, don't split any other pair.

Total of 9 or Less

When your hand has a total count of 9 or less, it cannot be busted and should, therefore, always be hit.

Total of 10 or 11

These hands also cannot be busted and should always be hit, but only when the dealer shows a 10 or ace. When the dealer shows a 9 or less, the chances of getting 20 or 21 and beating the dealer are very good. You should, therefore, take advantage of this by doubling down, which doubles your wager.

Total of 12 to 16

This is a stiff hand that *can* be busted, so you should stand if the dealer shows a 6 or less, in the hope that the dealer will bust. If the dealer shows a 7 or higher, she likely has a pat hand. In this case, you probably have a losing hand, so you should take a hit and risk busting in an attempt to beat the dealer. Continue hitting until your total count exceeds 16.

Total of 17 to 21

This is called a pat hand, and you should always stand. Although you may not have the dealer beat, your risk of busting is too high to take a hit. The exception is an ace 6 hand, which should be hit. A 17 is not a good total—the best it can do against a dealer's pat hand is push. Since, a soft 17 can't be busted, you have everything to gain and little to lose by hitting.

Insurance

Do not take the insurance side bet because the odds always favor the house. The aforementioned rules are summarized in the following chart:

A REALLY SIMPLE STRATEGY

PLAYER HAND	PLAYER ACTION
Pair Aces or 8s	Always SPLIT
Other pairs	Never split; play as regular hand
9 or less	Always HIT
10 or 11	DOUBLE if dealer shows 2 to 9 HIT if dealer shows 10 or Ace
12 to 16	STAND if dealer shows 6 or less HIT if dealer shows 7 or higher
17 to 21	Always STAND, except HIT A6

Never take insurance.

ABRIDGED BASIC STRATEGY

The next step-up in complexity is the **Abridged Basic Strategy**. Once you have learned the Really Simple Strategy, learning the Abridged Basic Strategy is an easy and worthwhile step to take, and you should take this step as soon as you can. The Abridged Basic Strategy will reduce the house advantage to about 1%.

As in the Really Simple Strategy, the surrender option has been omitted, but then, most casinos don't offer it anymore, anyway. A few odd splitting and doubling situations were also omitted.

All in all, the Abridged Basic Strategy modifies only about 7% of the rules in the full-blown Universal Basic Strategy.

When you apply the following rules, be sure to play non-split pairs like a hard hand, as the table indicates. If the strategy tells you to split a pair, then it is correct to resplit if you catch a third card of the same value. Finally, you can reduce the decision-making process to three steps, since there is no surrender rule to consider.

Pair of Aces
Always split a pair of aces. The value of the initial hand is either a 2 or a soft 12, neither of which is very good. By splitting, you end up with two chances of catching a 21.

Pair of 8s
Always split a pair of eights. The value of the initial hand is 16 (the worst hand you can have). By splitting the eights, you are bound to develop better hands. The idea is to limit your losses.

Pair of 2s, 3s, 6s, or 7s
Split these pairs only if the dealer shows a 2 through 7. Statistically, the initial totals of 4, 6, 12, or 14 are worse hands than when they are split. You should minimize losses by splitting when the dealer has a greater chance of busting.

Pair of 9s
Split the 9s only if the dealer shows a 2 through 7. Although a 9 is a pretty good starting card because it can turn into a 19, against a dealer upcard of 8 or higher,

doubling the bet is too risky and you should stand on the hard 18.

Pair of 4s

Never split fours. The total of 8 is a much better hand than the individual 4s, so you should keep it. Catching a 10 will give you an 18, which is not a great hand, but is much better than 14.

Pair of 5s

Never split 5s. The total of 10 has a good chance of hitting to a 20 or 21. Play a pair of 5s as a hard hand, which means you should double down against a dealer's 2 through 9, just as you would for a hard 10.

Pair of 10s

Never split ten-value cards. A 20 is an excellent pat hand that you should never break up.

Soft A-2 to A-6

Never stand on these hands; they are poor hands that can't be busted, so you should try to improve them by hitting.

Soft A-7 to A-9

Always stand because these are strong hands that are not likely to be improved with a hit. In the Universal Basic Strategy, the A-7 hand is treated differently, but here it is simplified.

Soft A-10

This, of course, is a natural for which you will get paid 3 to 2 if the dealer doesn't also have one.

Total of 5 to 9

Always hit a total count of 9 or less. Since these hands can't be busted, they should be hit regardless of the dealer upcard.

Total of 10 or 11

Double down when the dealer shows a 9 or less, otherwise hit. The chances of getting 20 or 21 are good, and this will usually beat a dealer with an upcard of 2 through 9.

Hard 12 to 16

Stand when the dealer shows a 6 or less, in the hope that the dealer will bust. A dealer upcard of 7 or higher indicates a possible pat hand, so you have to take a hit and risk busting in an attempt to beat the dealer's hand. Always continue hitting until your total count exceeds 16.

Hard 17 to 21

This is called a pat hand, and you should always stand. Although you may not have the dealer beat, your risk of busting is too high to take a hit.

Insurance

Do not take the insurance side bet because the odds favor the house.

These rules are summarized in the following chart:

ABRIDGED BASIC STRATEGY

PLAYER HAND	PLAYER ACTION
PAIRS	
8 or Ace	Always SPLIT
2, 3, 6, 7, or 9	SPLIT if dealer shows 2 to 7, else play as hard hand
4, 5, or 10	Never SPLIT; always play as hard hand
SOFT HANDS	
A-2 to A-6	Always HIT
A-7 to A-10	Always STAND
HARD HANDS	
5 to 9	Always HIT
10 or 11	DOUBLE if dealer shows 2 to 9; HIT on dealer 10 or Ace
12 to 16	STAND if dealer shows 2 to 6; HIT if dealer shows 7 to Ace
17 to 21	Always STAND

Never take insurance

6

THE UNIVERSAL BASIC STRATEGY

Early professional blackjack players learned that there was one right way and many wrong ways to play the game. By combining experience, sound reasoning, and their knowledge of odds, they developed winning playing strategies, which they applied very successfully. Only a select few people knew these strategies, however, and they intended to keep it that way.

During the early 1950s, Roger Baldwin, Wilbert Cantey, Herbert Maisel, and James McDermott, a group of sharp statistical analysts, published the first blackjack playing strategy in a mathematical journal. They applied their knowledge of statistical analysis to the game and after three years of plugging away on mechanical desk calculators, arrived at a surprisingly-accurate playing strategy. They called it the *basic strategy*, and the term has been with us ever since.

At that time, blackjack was only a moderately-popular game, so just a few people recognized the importance of their efforts. One of those people was Professor Edward O. Thorp of M.I.T. who, a few years later, refined their work using an IBM 704 computer. Professor Thorp then published the first book describing a method for winning at blackjack by keeping track of the played cards. The basic strategy was the backbone of his innovative card-counting system.

In the following years, Julian Braun and others developed computer programs that simulated millions of blackjack hands. These simulations ultimately brought the original basic strategy to perfection. This perfect basic strategy is what I am presenting here and in later chapters.

LEARNING THE UNIVERSAL BASIC STRATEGY

Now that you have memorized and practiced the Abridged Basic Strategy rules, you should be able to take on the full basic strategy. If you are not a card counter, basic strategy is the best way to play all blackjack hands. Therefore, to reduce the house advantage to the lowest possible percentage, it is necessary to slavishly follow every one of the prescribed instructions in the basic strategy.

When the blackjack game rules change from casino to casino, the basic strategy also changes. However, for most of the common rule changes, the corresponding modifications in basic strategy are very minor and those differences are given in later chapters.

This chapter covers the Universal Basic Strategy which, as the name implies, can be used with any multiple deck blackjack game that has normal game rules. Specifically, it is an almost exact strategy for the set of baseline game rules I have previously defined as the Standard Blackjack

Rules, which are also the rules used in Atlantic City. So that you don't have to thumb back in the book, these rules are repeated below.

STANDARD BASELINE BLACKJACK RULES
(ATLANTIC CITY)

1. Six- or eight-deck game.
2. Dealer must stand on all 17s.
3. Resplitting of pairs allowed (except aces).
4. Double down on any two cards.
5. Double down after splitting allowed.
6. Surrender is not an option.
7. All ties are pushes.
8. Natural pays 3 to 2.
9. Lose all to a dealer natural.

The Universal Basic Strategy is also a close approximation for games with slightly different rules. It can be effectively used for any multiple deck or CSM game with commonly found rules, such as the following.

1. Dealer must hit soft 17.
2. Double down on 10 or 11 only.
3. No double down after splitting.
4. Resplitting aces allowed.

THE UNIVERSAL BASIC STRATEGY

To ease the effort in memorizing the Universal Basic Strategy, it has been divided into three parts: (1) Pairs, (2) Soft Hands, and (3) Hard Hands. By taking on the project a part at a time, it shouldn't be too hard to handle.

PAIRS

Some pairs are always split, some are never split, and some are split only for certain dealer upcards. If it is correct to split a pair, then it is correct to resplit if you catch a third card of the same rank. Whenever you don't split a pair, play it as a hard hand.

Pair of 2s or 3s

Split 2s or 3s only when the dealer shows a 7 or less. A total of 4 or 6 is a worse hand than a 2 or 3, so by splitting we minimize losses when the dealer has a greater chance of busting. When the dealer shows an upcard of 8 or higher, indicating a likely pat hand, it is more prudent to play the pair as a hard hand rather than splitting and doubling the wager on a poor hand.

Pair of 4s

In most situations, a pair of 4s should not be split. The total of 8 is a much better starting hand than the individual 4s. Getting hit with a 10-value card will give you an 18, which is not a great hand, but is much better than a 14. In casinos where double down is allowed after a split, we take advantage of the weakest dealer upcards of 5 or 6 by splitting the 4s. If you play exclusively in casinos where double down is not permitted after splitting, you may wish to white-out the "P" in the dealer 5 and 6 columns and write an "H."

Pair of 5s

Never split 5s. A pair of 5s has a total value of 10, which is a very strong base hand with a good chance of hitting to a 20 or 21. If you split, you will end up with two weak hands that might even turn into terrible 15s. Always play a pair of 5s as a hard hand, which means you should double down against a dealer's 2 through 9, just as you would for a hard 10.

Pair of 6s

Split the 6s only when the dealer shows a 2 through 6. This is a poor hand no matter which way you go, so by splitting against the dealer's weakest upcards you limit your losses, and hope the dealer busts. If the dealer shows a 7 or higher, play the 12 as a hard hand (which means hit until you reach 17 or higher).

Pair of 7s

Split the 7s only when the dealer shows a 7 or less. This is not much better than 6s, but if you catch a 10 after you split, you will have 17. This is not great, but is better than 14. If the dealer shows an 8 or higher, grit your teeth and play the 14 as a hard hand.

Pair of 8s

Always split a pair of 8s. Again, the total value of 16 is the worst hand you can have. By splitting the 8s, you are bound to develop better hands. If you catch a 10, you will have 18, which is a whole lot better than 16. The point here is to minimize losses.

Pair of 9s

Split the 9s only when the dealer shows a 6 or less. This is not a bad hand, especially if you catch a 10 after you split. Against a dealer 7 or higher, however, doubling your bet by splitting is too risky and you should stand on the hard 18.

Pair of 10s

Never split 10-value cards. A 20 is an excellent hand, with a greater than 50-50 chance of winning regardless of the dealer's upcard. You should always stand. Yes, you will see some players split 10s. You will also see players hit a hard 19 or 20. That is why blackjack is such a profitable game for the casinos.

Pair of Aces

Always split a pair of aces. The value of the initial hand is either a 2 or a soft 12, neither of which is very good. Because of the predominance of 10s in the deck, the 2 can easily turn into a hard 12. By splitting, you end up with the best possible base cards, giving you two good chances of getting 21s. Remember that the dealer will give you just one card on each ace, and you cannot take any hits. If one of those cards is another ace, you should resplit to a third hand, if the casino permits you to do so.

UNIVERSAL BASIC STRATEGY
• Pairs •

Player's Hand	Dealer's Upcard									
	2	3	4	5	6	7	8	9	10	Ace
2-2	P	P	P	P	P	P	H	H	H	H
3-3	P	P	P	P	P	P	H	H	H	H
4-4	H	H	H	P	P	H	H	H	H	H
5-5	D	D	D	D	D	D	D	D	H	H
6-6	P	P	P	P	P	H	H	H	H	H
7-7	P	P	P	P	P	P	H	H	H	H
8-8	P	P	P	P	P	P	P	P	P	P
9-9	P	P	P	P	P	S	P	P	S	S
10-10	S	S	S	S	S	S	S	S	S	S
A-A	P	P	P	P	P	P	P	P	P	P

H = hit   S = stand   P = split pair   D = double down

SOFT HANDS

An initial hand that contains an ace is called *soft* because it can be hit with no risk of busting. If, after taking one or more hits, the ace can continue to be counted as 11 without busting, then the hand is still soft. With the ace taking on the dual value of 1 or 11, a soft hand is much more versatile than a hard hand and must be played differently.

Soft 13 or 14 (A-2 or A-3)

Double down when the dealer shows a 5 or 6, otherwise hit. If you are playing at a table where doubling is restricted, hit against all dealer upcards. Never stand on these hands. Since they can't be busted, you should try to improve them. Upcards of 5 and 6 are the dealer's worst hands with an excellent chance of busting, therefore, doubling is worthwhile even though your resulting hand will usually not be very good.

Soft 15 or 16 (A-4 or A-5)

Treat these the same way as soft 13 and 14, except double down against a dealer's 4 through 6. Again, at a table where doubling is restricted, hit against all dealer upcards. Never stand.

Soft 17 (A-6)

Double down when the dealer shows a 3 through 6, otherwise hit. Where doubling is restricted, hit against all dealer upcards. Because standing on a hard 17 is correct, many players think they should stand on soft 17 as well. It should be made clear that 17 is not a good total—the best it can do against a dealer's pat hand is push. The only reason for standing on a hard 17 is to avoid the high risk of busting. But, a soft 17 can't be busted, so you have everything to gain and little to lose by hitting.

Soft 18 (A-7)

Double down when the dealer shows a 3 through 6, hit when the dealer shows 9, 10, or ace, otherwise stand. Doubling against all the weakest dealer hands with a soft total of 18 is worthwhile because if the dealer doesn't bust, you may still win. Where doubling is restricted, stand against dealer upcards of 2 through 8.

Soft 19 through 21
(A-8 through A-10)

Always stand because these are strong hands that are not likely to be improved with a hit. Of course, the A-10 on the initial two cards is a natural.

UNIVERSAL BASIC STRATEGY
• Soft Hands •

Player's Hand	Dealer's Upcard									
	2	3	4	5	6	7	8	9	10	Ace
13 (A-2)	H	H	H	Dh	Dh	H	H	H	H	H
14 (A-3)	H	H	H	Dh	Dh	H	H	H	H	H
15 (A-4)	H	H	Dh	Dh	Dh	H	H	H	H	H
16 (A-5)	H	H	Dh	Dh	Dh	H	H	H	H	H
17 (A-6)	H	Dh	Dh	Dh	Dh	H	H	H	H	H
18 (A-7)	S	Ds	Ds	Ds	Ds	S	S	H	H	H
19 (A-8)	S	S	S	S	S	S	S	S	S	S
20 (A-9)	S	S	S	S	S	S	S	S	S	S
21 (A-10)	S	S	S	S	S	S	S	S	S	S

H = hit   S = stand
Dh = double down if allowed, else hit
Ds = double down if allowed, else stand

HARD HANDS

An initial hand that does not contain an ace and has a total count of 12 or more is called **hard** because the total numeric value of the hand is fixed and an additional card can cause it to exceed a count of 21. After taking one or more hits, any hand with an ace that has to be counted as 1 to keep from busting, is also a hard hand.

THE UNIVERSAL BASIC STRATEGY

Although, totals of 5 to 11 are not hard hands, I include them in this category for lack of a better place.

Total of 5 to 8
Always hit a total count of 8 or less. Since these hands can't be busted, they should be hit regardless of the dealer upcard. Never double down on 8 or less; it's too risky.

Total of 9
Double down when the dealer shows a 3 through 6, otherwise hit. Where doubling is restricted, hit against all dealer upcards. Doubling against the weakest dealer hands with a 9 is worthwhile because if the dealer doesn't bust, you may still win.

Total of 10
Double down for dealer upcards of 2 through 9, otherwise hit. When the dealer shows a 9 or less, the chances of getting 20 or 21 and beating the dealer are very good. Take advantage of this by doubling down.

Total of 11
Double down for dealer upcards of 2 through 10, other-wise hit. When the dealer shows a 10 or less, the chances of getting a 21 and beating the dealer are very good, so you should take advantage of this by doubling down.

Hard 12
Of all the stiff hands, this one has the least chance of being busted, so you should take a single hit when the dealer shows a 2 or 3. Also, hit until you reach 17 or more when the dealer has a strong upcard of 7 or higher. Stand when the dealer shows a 4, 5, or 6, and hope she busts.

Hard 13 to 16

These stiff hands can be busted easier than a 12, so you should stand when the dealer shows a 6 or less, in the hope that the dealer will bust. A dealer upcard of 7 or higher often indicates a pat hand, so you probably have a loser. Consequently, you have to take a hit and risk busting in an attempt to beat the dealer's hand. Continue hitting until your total count exceeds 16.

Hard 17 to 21

These are called pat hands, and you should always stand. Although you may not have the dealer beat, your risk of busting is too high to take a hit.

UNIVERSAL BASIC STRATEGY
• Hard Hands •

Player's Hand	Dealer's Upcard									
	2	3	4	5	6	7	8	9	10	Ace
5 to 8	H	H	H	H	H	H	H	H	H	H
9	H	Dh	Dh	Dh	Dh	H	H	H	H	H
10	Dh	Dh	Dh	Dh	Dh	Dh	Dh	Dh	H	H
11	Dh	Dh	Dh	Dh	Dh	Dh	Dh	Dh	Dh	H
12	H	H	S	S	S	H	H	H	H	H
13	S	S	S	S	S	H	H	H	H	H
14	S	S	S	S	S	H	H	H	H	H
15	S	S	S	S	S	H	H	H	H	H
16	S	S	S	S	S	H	H	H	H	H
17 to 21	S	S	S	S	S	S	S	S	S	S

H = hit   S = stand
Dh = double down if allowed, else hit

THE COMPLETE CHART

On the following page is the complete Universal Basic Strategy chart. It is simply an aggregate of the previous three charts, with one exception: the complete chart includes rules for what to do when you encounter the surrender option. The chart is arranged in the same decision order that you use to evaluate your hand: pairs, soft hands, hard hands.

When you play in a multiple deck blackjack game, your best results will always come when you religiously abide by the Universal Basic Strategy. Any deviations are at your own risk. The chart will also serve you well if, at some time, you decide to play in a single- or double-deck game. It is so close an approximation that it doesn't pay to memorize a second set of strategy rules.

Key to chart abbreviations:
H = hit   S = stand   P = split pair
Dh = double down if allowed, else hit
Ds = double down if allowed, else stand
Fh = surrender (fold) if allowed, or else hit

UNIVERSAL BASIC STRATEGY

Player's Hand	Dealer's Upcard									
	2	3	4	5	6	7	8	9	10	Ace
A-A	P	P	P	P	P	P	P	P	P	P
10-10	S	S	S	S	S	S	S	S	S	S
9-9	P	P	P	P	P	S	P	P	S	S
8-8	P	P	P	P	P	P	P	P	P	P
7-7	P	P	P	P	P	P	H	H	H	H
6-6	P	P	P	P	P	H	H	H	H	H
5-5	Dh	Dh	Dh	Dh	Dh	Dh	Dh	Dh	H	H
4-4	H	H	H	P	P	H	H	H	H	H
3-3	P	P	P	P	P	P	H	H	H	H
2-2	P	P	P	P	P	P	H	H	H	H
21(A-10)	S	S	S	S	S	S	S	S	S	S
20 (A-9)	S	S	S	S	S	S	S	S	S	S
19 (A-8)	S	S	S	S	S	S	S	S	S	S
18 (A-7)	S	Ds	Ds	Ds	Ds	S	S	H	H	H
17 (A-6)	H	Dh	Dh	Dh	Dh	H	H	H	H	H
16 (A-5)	H	H	Dh	Dh	Dh	H	H	H	H	H
15 (A-4)	H	H	Dh	Dh	Dh	H	H	H	H	H
14 (A-3)	H	H	H	Dh	Dh	H	H	H	H	H
13 (A-2)	H	H	H	Dh	Dh	H	H	H	H	H
17 - 21	S	S	S	S	S	S	S	S	S	S
16	S	S	S	S	S	H	H	Fh	Fh	Fh
15	S	S	S	S	S	H	H	H	Fh	H
14	S	S	S	S	S	H	H	H	H	H
13	S	S	S	S	S	H	H	H	H	H
12	H	H	S	S	S	H	H	H	H	H
11	Dh	Dh	Dh	Dh	Dh	Dh	Dh	Dh	Dh	H
10	Dh	Dh	Dh	Dh	Dh	Dh	Dh	Dh	H	H
9	H	Dh	Dh	Dh	Dh	H	H	H	H	H
5 - 8	H	H	H	H	H	H	H	H	H	H

7

PLAYING IN THE CASINO

Many people who take a vacation at a gambling venue, simply walk into a casino, find the nearest blackjack table with an empty seat, sit down and begin to play. A better approach is to first survey most of the tables in the casino in order to find the most suitable game. What you should look for is explained in the following sections.

TABLE LIMITS

It can be more than a little embarrassing to plop down at a table, throw down a fifty, ask for nickels, and then find out that the table has a hundred-dollar minimum bet limit. Every blackjack table has a little placard that gives the betting limits, and you should inspect those signs before you select a table. This sign usually looks like the following illustration:

TABLE LIMIT
Min $10 Max $1000

In many casinos, the minimum bet can be quickly determined by the color of the sign. Red indicates a $5 minimum, yellow indicates $10, green indicates $25, and black indicates $100. Sometimes the placard may also post one or more specific rules for that table, such as in the following examples:

TABLE LIMIT
Min $25 Max $2500
Double down on 10 or 11 only

TABLE LIMIT
Min $25 Max $2500
No double down after splitting

To determine how much you can afford to bet, be sure to read the next chapter on Money Management.

GAME RULES

Once you have settled on your betting limits, the next step is to find a table with decent playing rules. You can determine if the dealer hits or stands on a soft 17 by looking at the information imprinted on the felt tabletop. The other rule that is always imprinted is the insurance side bet. This rule is immaterial because (1) it never changes and (2) you should never take the insurance wager, as you have learned in the chapters on basic strategy.

So, what about the other rules? The slow way to find out is to watch the play of the game for a while; the fast way is to ask the dealer. Sometimes one or two rules are posted on the Table Limit placard.

PLAYING THE CASINO

Using the information in previous chapters, you should have no trouble finding a game with reasonable rules. Actually, if you just avoid games with outrageous rules, such as less than a 3 to 2 payoff for a natural, you will almost invariably be playing a game in which the house has significantly less than a 1% advantage.

PLAYING THE GAME

Now that you've found a table with suitable betting limits and reasonable playing rules, take a seat if there is one available. Except for some advanced playing techniques, which are beyond the scope of this book, it doesn't matter which seat you take. Most of the time, you won't have much choice. Unless you are sitting down at a high-limit table, there will probably be only one or two unoccupied seats to choose from. If you are a relative beginner and need extra time to decide how to play your hand, find a seat as close to third base as you can.

Placing a Wager

The dealer will not give you any cards until you have put a wager in the betting box in front of you. You are not allowed to touch your bet after the cards have been dealt. Once the hand is over, and the dealer has paid the winners, you can remove your chips and place another bet.

Sometimes, when you first sit down, a dealer will not deal you a hand until after the next shuffle. This is done to thwart *back counters*. A **back counter** is a card counter who loiters near a blackjack table keeping track of the count without actually playing. When the count turns favorable, he takes a seat and bets heavily. Casinos don't like card counters, and they especially hate back counters.

CSMs were specifically designed to foil all card counters, so you can always sit down at a CSM table and begin playing right away.

Since you will be a basic strategy player, a CSM table is as suitable for you as a conventional multiple deck game.

Dealing the Hand

As you have learned, once all the bets have been placed, the dealer gives each player two face-up cards and gives herself one face-up card and one facedown card. If the dealer's upcard is an ace or a 10-value card, she checks her hole card to see if she has a natural (but not in Atlantic City). If she has a natural, everyone who does not also have a natural loses, and the hand is over. Variations of this procedure were covered in a previous chapter.

Playing the Hand

If the dealer does not have a natural, the play of the game continues. Starting at the first occupied seat to the left of the dealer (first base), each player gets an opportunity to act on his hand. Whenever a player's hand is busted, the dealer immediately removes that player's cards and bet. When all the players are finished, the dealer turns over her hole card and plays her own hand according to the casino rules previously described. She then collects the losing wagers and pays the winners.

Player Signals

Blackjack in the United States is basically a silent game. That is, you rarely have to say anything to the dealer. If you need a hit, you either point at your cards or tap the felt with your index finger, and if you want to stand, you wave your hand over the cards. In a face-up game, never touch any cards.

If you want to split or double down, place another bet alongside your initial bet. Most of the time, the dealer will know exactly which action you want to take. If she isn't sure, she will ask you.

About the only time you have to say anything is when you want to surrender (assuming it is an option). Simply say "surrender" when it is your turn.

Most European countries don't recognize hand signals in their blackjack games. Before you sit down at a table, it is best to hang around for a while until you learn the foreign terminology for hitting, standing, splitting, and doubling.

TABLE ETIQUETTE

At the start of each hand, you must put a wager in the betting box. If you are slow in doing this, most dealers will gently remind you, but it will also hold up the game. Some dealers may assume that you intend to sit out that round and bypass you entirely on the deal.

Once the dealer starts distributing the cards, you may not touch your original bet. If you do, you will be admonished. This is because one method of cheating is to change the amount of the bet after seeing how good a hand was dealt.

Whenever the players' initial cards are dealt face up, which is true for all multiple deck and CSM games, you must never touch your cards. The dealer does all the card handling. This is another anti-cheating rule.

Avoid commenting on a stranger's hand or his playing actions. Doing this will only bring you grief and resentment. Most players think they know how to play well and don't appreciate criticism—especially from a stranger. If someone does that to you, either ignore them or try to make light of it.

If you are seated at third base, you must be a little thick-skinned. Some gamblers think that because it is the last hand before the dealer plays, the third baser must play his hand correctly or the dealer will win more often. "Hey, that king you got would have caused the dealer to bust!" is a typical comment. As though you knew what the next card was going to be! The fact is, the third-base player's actions will hurt the dealer as often as it helps her, no matter how badly he plays his hand.

The third-base position is even worse in Germany. There, most gamblers think it is that player's *responsibility* to try and give the dealer a bad hand even at the expense of his own hand. Of course, nobody seems able to explain how the player is supposed to know the value of the next card. I always thought Germans were so logical!

TIPPING

Let me say at the outset that I don't believe in tipping unless a service has been rendered in an efficient and pleasant manner. In a casino, tipping is never required. You are in total control as to when, where, and how much to tip.

Something many people are unaware of is that if you give a table dealer a generous tip, that tip will be shared with the other table dealers on that shift. To comply with IRS regulations, the tips must be pooled and taxes withheld by the casino before the remaining money is divided among the other dealers. So your big tip is first taxed and then the balance is split up evenly between all the table dealers in that pit. This doesn't seem to bother some people, but it bothers me.

In a restaurant, the tipping situation is well defined. The 15% to 20% tip has become so standardized that many patrons leave 15% or 20% whether the service was good, bad, or mediocre. In a casino, however, there are large gray areas. So much so that many people overtip when tipping isn't even indicated.

Remember that the blackjack dealer is an employee of the casino, and her job is to separate you from your money. She is on the opposite side of the table. She is your opponent. Any dealer who doesn't always look out for the interests of the casino will, sooner or later, lose her job.

Expert and professional card players tip dealers for good will and for extraordinary services. These services might include dealing a deck down further than usual to benefit a card counter or might be in the form of subtle hints on whether or not to take a hit. In other words, they tip because the dealer actually helped them to win money. I would tip a dealer only after a run of good luck, and then only if she were a pleasant, helpful person and I enjoyed playing at her table.

Tipping while losing or breaking even is a waste of money. So is tipping a surly or hostile dealer.

8

GENERAL PLAYING ADVICE

Some people who think they know more than the experts have a tendency to do things in a half-cocked manner and then wonder why they keep losing money. This chapter is designed to discourage you from doing dumb things. It begins with the most important advice I can give to beginning players: practice, practice, practice.

PRACTICE, PRACTICE, PRACTICE

The secret to learning basic strategy is to practice, and practice some more—*before* you enter a casino and begin to risk real money. There are several ways to do this. You can gather together your family or a few friends and play for buttons or matchsticks.

When you do this, always play by casino rules rather than home-game rules.

Actually, all you need is a deck of cards and you can play all by yourself. You first function as the dealer and dole out several players' hands. Then switch hats and act on each player's hand, in turn. When the player's hands are finished, you become the dealer again and play your hand according to the casino rules. If you own a home computer, it gets even simpler. There is plenty of blackjack software available that will let you play hands rapidly without shuffling delays.

BAD PLAYING STRATEGIES

One good way to lose money while playing blackjack is to employ a bad strategy. This is especially inexcusable when you know the correct strategy, but as I said earlier, some people think they know better.

Two bad playing strategies often used by novice players seem to have a certain logic. They are "mimic the dealer" and "never bust." Even some basic strategy players have reverted to one of these during an extended losing streak. Sometimes these strategies seem to work for a while, but in the long run the house picks up a large advantage.

Mimic the Dealer

Since the dealer wins most of the time by hitting 16 and standing on 17, it is obviously the best playing strategy. Shouldn't I do the same? Absolutely not! When you mimic the dealer, you are not doing yourself any favors, but you are doing the house a big favor. The dealer doesn't win most of the time because she hits 16 and stands on 17, she wins because she plays her hand *last*. Consequently, when you bust, you always lose, and when the dealer busts, she only loses if you didn't bust first. This is such a large advantage for the dealer that if you try to mimic her, the house edge rises to almost 5.5%.

Never Bust

Since I lose when I bust, even if the dealer busts, wouldn't I be better off never hitting a 12 or higher? Then I would win whenever the dealer busts.

Good try, but this is another way of rapidly thinning out your bankroll. On average, the dealer busts less than 29% of the time. That means you will be guaranteed a win on almost 29% of your hands. But what about the other 71%? When the dealer doesn't bust, it means she achieved a total count of 17 through 21—and she did that over 71% of the time. Every time you stand on a low count and the dealer doesn't bust, you lose.

In fact, if you don't achieve an average count of 19 when the dealer shows a 7 or higher, you will lose most of the time. Using a no-bust strategy will increase the house edge to almost 4%.

TEN WORST PLAYING ERRORS

It is amazing how many players who are familiar with correct basic strategy are reluctant to make certain indicated plays. Whenever you don't follow the basic strategy playing rules, you will lose money in the long run. Yes, you may guess right occasionally, but if you follow your own imperfect intuition you will always end up losing more than you gain. The ten hands listed below seem to be the ones most often played incorrectly.

Hit an Ace-Ace Against a Dealer 10

This hand should always be SPLIT. No matter how you look at it, a hand of 2 or 12 is not good. So why are some players reluctant to split? Because they get only one card on each ace. What they don't understand is that the house allows only a single hit because it is such a strong play. It is exactly the same as getting one card when you double down on an 11, which is a good play—except that with split aces you have *two* good plays.

Stand on an Ace-6 Against a Dealer 7

Always HIT this hand. Unless the dealer busts, the best you can do is push. However, with a 7 showing, the dealer will bust only 26% of the time. When you hit you cannot bust and you may improve the hand. Never stand.

Stand on an Ace-7 Against a Dealer 9

Always HIT this hand. Why hit a perfectly good 18? Because, contrary to popular belief, 18 is not a good hand, especially when the dealer shows a 9 or better. With a 9 upcard, the dealer will bust only 23% of the time and will beat your hand over 50% of the time. You must try to improve your holding. Never stand.

Stand on an Ace-7 Against a Dealer 10

Be sure to HIT this hand. Another perfectly good 18? Of course not! Not when the dealer will win over 56% of the time. Hit it!

Stand on a 9-9 Against a Dealer 9

Always SPLIT this hand. If you stand on this 18, it is no different than standing on an ace 7: the dealer will beat you more than 50% of the time. Splitting gives you a better chance of winning.

Hit (or stand) on an 8-8 Against a Dealer 10

Always SPLIT this hand. No matter what you do, it is a loser. Normally, a 16 is the worst hand you can get. At least, when it comes as a pair of 8s, you have the opportunity to improve it slightly. Of the available options, splitting loses the least money—*even though you doubled the bet!*

Hit (or stand) on 8-8 Against a Dealer Ace

Always SPLIT this hand. This is essentially the same situation as above, and splitting is your best option.

Hit an 11 Against a Dealer 10

DOUBLE this hand. Getting a count of 11 in the first two cards is a winning situation. That's when you take advantage and double down, just as the basic strategy tells you to do.

Stand on a 12 Against a Dealer 3

HIT this hand. This is also a losing hand, but you will limit your losses when you hit, although not by much.

Stand on a 12 Against a Dealer 2

HIT this hand. Just like the above hand, you must take a hit to limit your losses.

CHEATING

Cheating is a controversial subject over which there is quite a bit of disagreement. There are, of course, two sides to the question: (1) Casinos cheating the players and (2) players cheating the casinos.

If you plan on cheating a casino, that is entirely your decision. Just be aware of the risks, and be aware of the severity of the consequences if you are caught.

As far as casinos cheating the players, it does happen, but very seldom in the major gambling venues. When it happens, it is usually the action of an individual dealer. Dealers cheat for any number of reasons, but one of the most common is that they are actually stealing from the casino. To avert suspicion, they then cheat the players to assure that the table drop on their shift is normal.

Cheating by card manipulation is almost entirely confined to hand-dealt games. Dealers rarely cheat individual players. Most cheating dealers simply give themselves good hands, cheating all the players at their table.

Cheating with a dealing shoe is possible, but it requires the use of a specially-rigged shoe. It is so difficult and risky to get a rigged shoe into play without the help of management that it is rarely done in legal casinos. Furthermore, any casino caught using such a shoe would face a long license suspension. Thus, if you are playing at a multiple deck blackjack game, dealer cheating should be of no concern—so you needn't worry about it.

CARD COUNTING

As I have already said, card counting techniques are not covered in this book. With diligent practice, however, you may eventually become an expert basic strategy player. You know you have arrived when the correct basic strategy play becomes second nature and you rarely make a mistake. Once you have reached that point, you may want to try your hand at counting cards.

MONEY MANAGEMENT

The purpose of applying the basic strategy when playing blackjack is to make money. The purpose of money management is to retain as much of that money as possible. After you have won a sum of money as the result of diligence and intelligent play, you should reap the rewards that those winnings can provide. Too many gamblers win a pile just to fritter it away by losing it back to the casino or giving it to the IRS. Hopefully, the advice in this chapter will help you to avoid those money traps.

PERSONAL BETTING LIMITS

You should determine ahead of time how much you can afford to bet. Blackjack is a rather volatile game, which means you may lose several hands before you start winning (or vice versa). If you want to stay alive for any length of time, you should not sit down at a $25 minimum table with only $200 in your pocket. A losing split and a couple of bad double downs will break you very quickly. How much, then, do you need to weather the ups and downs?

As a general rule of thumb, you should have a gambling bankroll of twenty to forty times your basic wager for your initial playing session. Why such a wide range for the bankroll? Because some people are more conservative than others, and this is just a guideline. You will have to determine the exact risk for yourself.

Let's say you have allocated $400 for a gambling session. The suggested betting range would then be $10 to $20 since the bankroll should be twenty to forty times your basic wager. This amount is calculated by dividing the total bankroll of $400 by forty to get $10 and by twenty for the $20. Thus, with a $400 bankroll, you shouldn't place an initial bet of more than $10 to $20 a hand. If, during your first playing session, you come out ahead, you can then readjust your betting level.

CONTROLLING YOUR BANKROLL

Before you sit down at any blackjack table, be sure you have first designated a specific sum of money to risk for your playing session. Otherwise, you may end up like some impromptu gamblers who, after sustaining a losing streak, continue to dig for more money in an attempt to recoup their losses. By doing this, they may eventually lose their entire bankroll during the first day of a gambling trip, and then wonder what they are going to do the rest of the time. Some will head for the nearest ATM and start using money that was never intended for gambling.

To avoid such a situation, let's say you are on a three-day gambling junket and have allocated $1500 that you can afford to lose. Divide that bankroll into three $500 stakes, one stake for each day. Whatever you do, don't gamble away more than $500 in any one day, and stay away from the ATMs. You must be disciplined about this.

> **IMPORTANT NOTE:** *If you can't maintain that kind of money discipline, you have a problem and should seek help. Although they would rather not, most casinos will tell you where to go or who to call to get the necessary help. If you don't do this, you can ruin your life.*

If your discipline is marginal, bring only the designated $500 with you into the casino. Leave the rest of it with someone you trust or lock it up in the room safe. If you lose the entire $500 stake, quit gambling for the day. Go sight-seeing, see a show, have dinner, but don't gamble another cent until the following day.

The next day, repeat the procedure with the second $500, but try not to lose it all this time. If you did lose your daily stake on the first day, you should carefully read the section on When to Quit, below.

By dividing your allocated gambling funds into daily stakes, you are maintaining a measure of control over your bankroll. Even if you do eventually lose it all, this form of monetary discipline will assure that you can do some gambling every day, which is the reason you went on the trip in the first place.

WHEN TO QUIT
The gambler who doesn't know when to quit will never come out ahead, no matter how well he plays. A commonly-heard piece of advice is: "Quit while you are

ahead." That's good advice, except that many people misinterpret it to mean: "Quit while you are winning." No, no, no! The correct rule is:

> ## *NEVER QUIT WHILE YOU ARE WINNING!*

When you get on a hot winning streak, you should always stick with it and slowly increase your bet size. Of course, you never know in advance when the streak will end, but sooner or later it will. When you do start losing, cut the size of your bets right down to the minimum, and if you continue to lose, quit playing. In other words:

> ## *QUIT ONLY WHEN YOU ARE LOSING!*

What if you win a few and lose a few, and the house is slowly grinding down your bankroll? Once you realize what is happening, take a break or at least change tables before you lose your entire daily stake. If you maintain the proper discipline, whenever you have gone through your daily gambling allotment, you are through gambling for the day.

Whatever you do, never try to recoup losses by increasing your bet size. Risking more money will not change your luck or change the inherent odds of the game you are playing. If you are on a losing streak, bigger bets will only cause you to lose faster.

You need to recognize those specific situations when your best option is to quit playing. Although there are some situations that you will have to determine for yourself, the following list covers most of them:

WHEN TO QUIT PLAYING

- When you are losing.
- When you decide that your intuition is better than basic strategy.
- When you are unhappy with the dealer.
- When you are unhappy with one or more players.
- When you are angry, for whatever reason.
- When you are depressed.
- When you are not feeling well.
- When you are tired.

If you are on a winning streak, however, grit your teeth and stick with it, even if you are unhappy, angry, or tired. Remember: *Never quit while you are winning!*

FIVE MONEY MANAGEMENT REMINDERS

1. Never play with money that you can't afford to lose—your chances of losing are greater than your chances of winning.

2. Never sit down at a blackjack table without first having designated specific funds for your gambling session.

3. Never change your pre-established bankroll rules and dig for more money if you lose your allocated stake for the session or for the day. Instead, quit playing.

4. Never deviate from the proper basic strategy playing rules.

5. Never try to chase your losses.

DEALING WITH THE IRS

The relationship between gambling and the IRS is a complex subject that even confounds lawyers and accountants specializing in taxes. In this section, I am not giving you any specific tax or legal advice, but only making you aware of certain IRS requirements. It is valuable to know about some of these things before encountering them in a real situation.

If you engage in casino transactions of more than $10,000, you should consult an accountant familiar with gaming laws. Casinos must report all cash transactions in excess of $10,000 to the IRS. They must also report an aggregate of cash transactions that occur within a 24-hour period and total more than $10,000. If you place a large bet at a sports book, cash-in chips, or even cash a check larger than $10,000, it must be reported. This is just a reporting requirement (presumably to control money laundering) and doesn't mean you have to pay taxes on the transaction. The state of Nevada also has a similar reporting requirement.

The IRS rule that is most important to gamblers is the requirement for the casino to report any lump sum win of $1200 or more by submitting a W-2G form. This, of course, refers mainly to slot machine jackpots, keno payouts, bingo prizes, and the like. Ordinary blackjack players don't have to worry about this requirement.

If you won a lump sum during a blackjack tournament, however, the IRS reporting requirement drops to $600. For this kind of a win, the casino has to submit a 1099-MISC form.

You would have to be a very heavy better to win $1200 in one hand, and you might lose it all on the next hand. The casino is not required to keep track of a blackjack player's wins and losses, so if you are a big better, it would be prudent to keep your own record. The casino is not required to withhold taxes unless the net winnings exceed $5000 or a payoff is at least 300 times the amount of the wager, which can't happen in blackjack.

Gambling winnings are considered ordinary income by the IRS and must be reported under "Other Income" on your 1040 tax return. If you are unfortunate enough to have a casino report your winnings, be sure you attach a copy of the W-2G or 1099-MISC to your return, or you will eventually get a letter from the IRS asking where it is.

If you are saddled with reported wins, you can reduce the tax burden (up to the amount of your winnings) if you can prove that you had offsetting gambling losses in the same year. Such losses cannot be subtracted from itemized winnings, but must be listed separately on Schedule A under "Miscellaneous Deductions." However, if your itemized deductions don't exceed the standard deduction, your gambling losses will not be useful as an offset. Also, keep in mind that you cannot reduce your overall tax by taking a *net* gambling loss—you can only offset winnings.

How do you prove that you had gambling losses? By keeping a detailed dairy of all your gambling activities. How detailed? The IRS recommendation is that you record the date, the time, the amount of your wins and losses, and the type of game. You should also record the name and location of the casino, and the names of any people (witnesses) with you at the time. Supporting documentation such as airline ticket receipts and hotel bills will help to convince an IRS auditor that you were actually there. However, unless you are a professional in the business of gambling *and* your trip was primarily for business purposes, do not try to deduct expenses such as transportation, hotel rooms, or restaurants.

Once you get used to the idea, you will see that keeping a diary is not as daunting as it first appears. How you actually deal with it, that is, what you put in and what you leave out, is entirely your decision. Just keep in mind that if the entire diary does not appear to be reasonable, an auditor may judge that it is inaccurate and disallow it.

If you gamble and lose money in a legal casino, you must pay taxes on any net winnings, but are not permitted to deduct a net gambling loss. This is a one-sided proposition, since it is obvious that the vast majority of recreational gamblers are net losers. How else could the gaming industry have built all those expensive hotels? It is no great wonder that some gamblers try to conceal their meager winnings.

10

STRATEGIES FOR RULE VARIATIONS

As I explained earlier, the Universal Basic Strategy is quite accurate for all the common rule variations, and if that works well enough for you then you should stick with it. When you are ready to pick up every tenth of a percent advantage in your game, however, you may want to become familiar with the small changes in strategy that maximize the return for every rule variation.

The rules covered in this chapter are variances from the Standard Blackjack Rules that I previously defined in this book. As you recall, these rules are the same as those used in Atlantic City. For your convenience, they are repeated below.

STANDARD BLACKJACK RULES
(ATLANTIC CITY)

1. Six- or eight-deck game.
2. Dealer must stand on all 17s.
3. Resplitting of pairs allowed (except aces).
4. Double down on any two cards.
5. Double down after splitting allowed.
6. Surrender not an option.
7. All ties are pushes.
8. Natural pays 3 to 2.
9. Lose all to a dealer natural.

In this chapter, I take no liberties. All the strategies are exact, so that the house edge is always reduced to the smallest possible percentage. In most cases, however, the differences are relatively minor and easy to remember.

DOUBLE DOWN NOT ALLOWED AFTER A SPLIT

Many casinos do not allow you to double down after splitting. This rule increases the house edge by a little more than 0.1%. Using the exact strategy for this rule, however, gives you only a very minimal gain over using the Universal Basic Strategy. The strategy adjustment requires only a few changes in pair splitting, as shown in the following chart:

Differences from Universal Basic Strategy when
DOUBLE DOWN IS NOT ALLOWED AFTER A SPLIT
Other Standard Blackjack Rules are unchanged

Player's Hand	Dealer's Upcard									
	2	3	4	5	6	7	8	9	10	Ace
Pair										
2-2	H	H								
3-3	H	H								
4-4				H	H					
6-6	H									

DEALER MUST HIT SOFT 17

The rule that a dealer must hit soft 17 has become prevalent in many casinos. The casinos like the rule because it increases their edge by 0.2%. Using the exact strategy for this rule, however, provides a very minimal gain over using the Universal Basic Strategy. The strategy adjustment requires only three changes for doubling and three changes for surrender, as shown in the following abbreviated chart:

Differences from Universal Basic Strategy when

DEALER MUST HIT SOFT 17

Other Standard Blackjack Rules are unchanged.

Player's Hand	Dealer's Upcard									
	2	3	4	5	6	7	8	9	10	Ace
Pair										
8-8										Fspl
Soft										
18 (A-7)	Ds									
19 (A-8)				Ds						
Hard										
11										Dh
15										Fh
17										Fs

Dh: Double down if allowed, else hit
Ds: Double down if allowed, else stand
Fh: Surrender if allowed, else hit
Fs: Surrender if allowed, else stand
Fspl: Surrender if allowed, else split

LOSE ALL TO A NATURAL

In the not too distant past, whenever the dealer dealt herself an ace or 10 upcard, she would immediately check her hole card to see if she had a natural. If she did, the hand was over and everyone automatically lost (except someone with another natural). Since the dealer's natural was settled at the beginning of the round, the players never had an opportunity to increase their bets by doubling or splitting. Consequently, any player who didn't also have a natural only lost his initial wager.

To eliminate another source of cheating, many casinos have changed the rule so that the dealer no longer checks for a natural at the start of a round. When the dealer doesn't peek at the hole card (or it is not dealt) until all the players have acted on their hands, a dealer's natural is not evident until all the hands have been played out. What about those players who increased their bets by doubling or splitting? In Atlantic City and other places in the United States where this procedure is used, the extra bets are ignored and the players only lose their initial wagers.

In Europe and Australia, however, all increased bets made as a result of doubling and splitting are lost to a dealer's natural. Because this is prevalent in Europe, it is called the European No-Hole-Card Rule.

By using the correct playing strategy, the casino's gain can be reduced to about 0.1%. The correct strategy is fairly obvious: don't split or double down against a dealer upcard of ace or 10. There is one exception, however. You should still split a pair of aces against a dealer 10.

Lose All to a Natural

Never split or double when
dealer shows an ace or 10.
EXCEPT
Split aces when dealer shows a 10.

11

BLACKJACK SIDE BETS

The casinos and casino suppliers have devised many different blackjack side bets for the purpose of increasing profits. A large sampling of these side bets is described below, mainly to show you that none of them are worth risking any money on. The house edge ranges from 3.8% to over 38%.

If you encounter a blackjack side bet that is not listed below, you can assume the house edge falls in the same range.

FIELD BET

In a field bet, you are betting that your first two cards will be a total of 12 through 16. If you get an ace-ace or an 8-8, the payout is double. The house edge for a field bet is 8.9%. Enough said.

INSURANCE

Insurance is a side bet that is offered at just about every casino blackjack game. You are betting that the dealer has a natural, in which case all insurance bets are paid off at 2 to 1 odds. If the dealer does not have a natural, the insurance side bet is lost.

When the undealt cards are sufficiently ten-rich, a card counter will take the insurance bet. A basic strategy player, however, should never take the bet. In a six- or eight-deck game, the house edge on the insurance bet is more than 7%. Suppose you have a natural—don't you want to protect it with insurance? No you don't! When you insure a natural, you are trading a 3 to 2 payoff most of the time for a 1 to 1 payoff all the time. Even then the house still has the edge, although it is much less.

OVER/UNDER 13

You are betting that your first two cards will total either over 13 or under 13, with aces counting as 1. If you get exactly 13, you lose either bet. The house edge on the "over" bet is 6.5%, and on the "under" bet is 10%. You decide which one to risk your money on, and I hope you decide that neither one is a good bet.

PAIR SQUARE

You are betting that your first two cards will be a pair. A pair pays 10 to 1 if it is unsuited and pays 15 to 1 if both cards are the same suit. Obviously, a same-suited pair can't happen in a single-deck game. In a six- or eight-deck game, the house edge is over 9%.

PROGRESSIVE BLACKJACK

Progressive Blackjack is a copyrighted game distributed by Mikohn Gaming. Other than the progressive side bet, it is a standard blackjack game. The $1 optional side bet gives you a chance of winning a bonus or the progressive jackpot when you are dealt one or more aces, in accordance with the following schedule:

PROGRESSIVE BLACKJACK

HAND	PAYS
1 Ace	$3
2 Aces (mixed suits)	$15
2 Aces (same suit)	$50
3 Aces (mixed suits)	$200
3 Aces (same suit)	$1000
4 Aces	$2000
4 Aces (same color)	Jackpot

These aces have to be the first cards dealt to your hand with no intervening non-aces. In other words, to win the $3 bonus, the ace has to be the first card you are dealt. To win the $15 bonus, the first two cards dealt to your hand have to be aces; to win the $200 bonus, the first three cards dealt have to be aces, and so forth.

Whenever it is won, the progressive jackpot is reset to $25,000. The house advantage depends on the value of the progressive jackpot. At the reset level, the house edge is a ridiculous 38.9%. When the progressive meter reaches $100,000, the house edge drops to about 20%. For the house edge to finally get to zero, the progressive jackpot has to exceed $207,000!

RED/BLACK

In this side bet, you wager on the color of the dealer's upcard—either red or black. The casino's edge comes into play when the dealer shows a deuce of your color. In that case, your bet is a push. The house edge is 3.8%, which is better than most side bets.

ROYAL MATCH

If you make this side bet, you will win a bonus if your first two cards are the same suit, which is called an Easy Match. If the two cards are a king and queen of the same suit, you win a bigger bonus. This is called a Royal Match. The following chart shows the payoffs.

ROYAL MATCH	
HAND	**PAYS**
Easy Match	2.5 to 1
Royal Match	25 to 1

For a six- or eight-deck game, the house edge is about 6.5%. In some casinos there is an additional bonus of $1000 if both the dealer and player have a Royal Match, reducing the house edge to around 6%.

STREAK

In this optional side bet, you place a wager on how many consecutive hands you might win. You can bet on a winning streak of two, three, four, or five hands, and if you make it, you will get paid according to the following schedule.

STREAK	
NO. OF WINS	**PAYS**
Two	3 to 1
Three	7 to 1
Four	17 to 1
Five	37 to 1

With a house edge ranging from 8% to 14%, you probably don't want to try this one.

SUPER SEVENS

When you make this optional side bet, you are hoping to get one or more 7s so that you get paid according to the following schedule:

SUPER SEVENS	
HAND	**PAYS**
First card any 7	3 to 1
First two cards unsuited 7s	50 to 1
First two cards suited 7s	100 to 1
First three cards unsuited 7s	500 to 1
First three cards suited 7s	5000 to 1

Regardless of the seemingly-high payouts, the house edge is still over 11%, making it a bad bet.

12

UNCONVENTIONAL BLACKJACK GAMES

In an attempt to lure players away from standard black-jack to similar games that are more profitable, casinos have devised a number of modifications. One of the oldest is *Double Exposure*, in which the enticement is that both of the dealer's cards are exposed at the start of each hand. Then there is *Spanish 21*, a multiple deck game with super-liberal rules and bonuses. The most recent blackjack modification is *Super Fun 21*, which is a copyrighted single-deck game with liberal rules. Of course, since the casinos expect to make a profit, all of these games have ways of sticking it to the player, some of which are not immediately obvious.

In general, these modified blackjack games have been money-makers for the casinos, mainly because most players use incorrect strategy. With correct playing strategy, however, the house edge is not unreasonable, usually staying under 1%. The only problem is that you have to learn another set of strategy rules. In the chapters that follow, I describe three modified blackjack games that require special playing strategies.

In this chapter, I cover two interesting blackjack variations that don't have the disadvantage of requiring a new strategy.

They are called *Multiple Action Blackjack* and *Twin Blackjack.*

MULTIPLE ACTION BLACKJACK

Multiple Action Blackjack, sometimes called Triple Action, is like playing three separate blackjack hands, except that you get dealt only one hand and play against three different dealer hands. At each player's position, there are three betting circles so that you can place one, two, or three bets. If you place only one bet, the game is identical to standard blackjack, and you play only against the first dealer hand. If you place two or three bets, you play your solitary hand against two or three different dealer hands.

Once the bets are down, the dealer gives each player two face-up cards and gives herself one upcard. After all the players are done acting on their hands, the dealer gives herself a second card and plays her hand just as in a standard blackjack game. At this point, the bet in the first circle is at risk and the dealer pays the winners and collects from the losers. If a player busts, however, all three bets are lost.

When the first round is finished, the dealer discards her draw cards, and retains her original upcard. Since the players based their playing strategies on that upcard, this keeps the game fair. All non-busted player hands remain in place. The dealer then draws new cards to complete a second dealer hand and compares it to the active player hands. Now, the bet in the second circle (if any) is at risk and the dealer again pays the winners and collects from the losers. This procedure is repeated a third time, after which all the cards are removed from the table and the players place their bets for a new game.

For example, let's say you put $10 in each betting circle. You are dealt a 9 and a king, and the dealer shows a 7. You happily stand on your 19. The dealer draws a 6 for a total of 13, and must draw again. The next card is an 8 for a total of 21, which beats your 19, so you lose your first bet.

After the dealer collects your $10 from the first betting circle, she discards her draw cards and retains the 7. She draws a 10 for a total of 17, which loses to your 19. You win your second bet and the dealer pays you $10. She now discards the 10 draw card and, again, retains the 7. On the third round, her first draw is a 5 for a total of 12, so she has to draw another card. The second card is a queen, causing the dealer to bust. You win the third round and are paid $10.

Just like in standard blackjack, you may split a pair. If you do, however, you must double each of your original bets. When the dealer shows an ace, you may take insurance on any or all of your initial bets (taking insurance is never recommended).

When doubling down, you have the option of doubling any or all of your bets. If you are following basic strategy and doubling is the correct action, you should double all your bets. Should you be fortunate enough to get a natural, each of your bets will be paid off at 3 to 2, assuming the dealer doesn't also get a natural.

Many players like Multiple Action Blackjack because with three bets on the table, a streak of good hands will win more money than in standard blackjack. Of course, this also involves risking more money. Another positive feature is that when the casinos are crowded, the betting limits at Multiple Action tables are usually lower than at standard blackjack tables.

Strategy:

Since Multiple Action Blackjack follows standard blackjack rules, you should play exactly according to the Universal Basic Strategy rules, or the abridged version. When you do this, the house edge is the same as for standard multiple deck blackjack.

Because of the risk of busting on all three bets, many players are reluctant to hit a 14, 15, or 16 when the dealer shows a 7 or higher. This is a serious mistake, which increases the casino's edge, and is one of the reasons the casinos like the game. Some players start with one or two bets and go to three bets if they are winning. Although this will reduce the volatility of the game, it will have no effect on the overall house edge.

TWIN BLACKJACK

As you might have guessed, in Twin Blackjack there are two betting spots, and each player is dealt two hands. Except for the fact that there are special bonuses, and less favorable rules to compensate for the bonuses, it is very similar to playing two hands in a standard multiple deck blackjack game.

Although a player has the choice of betting one or two hands, the bonuses only work for two hands. Whenever a player gets simultaneous naturals in both hands, it is called "twin blackjacks" and each one pays 2 to 1. If the simultaneous naturals contain identical cards, it is called "identical twin blackjacks" and each one pays 4 to 1. Don't hold your breath, however, because the chance of getting a pair of identical naturals is about 40,000 to 1.

To compensate for the bonuses, you are only allowed to resplit one time and you cannot double down after splitting. Even so, with correct play, the house edge is similar to standard multiple deck games.

Strategy:
Since Twin Blackjack pretty much follows standard blackjack rules, you should play exactly according to the Universal Basic Strategy, or the abridged version. When you correctly apply the Universal Basic Strategy, the house edge is about 0.44%. This is almost exactly the same edge as for an Atlantic City eight-deck game.

13

DOUBLE EXPOSURE

Double Exposure originated at Vegas World (the original name of the Stratosphere) in 1979, when Bob Stupak owned it. Since then, it has spread to several other casinos in Las Vegas, Atlantic City, and Mississippi. Although Double Exposure is the common name for this game, it is occasionally called Face Up 21 or Dealer Disclosure.

The distinguishing feature of this multiple deck game is that both of the dealer's initial cards are dealt face up. This gives the player a major strategic advantage, which is compensated by the following detrimental rules:

- Dealer wins all ties, except for a player natural
- Natural pays even money (instead of 3 to 2)
- Player may not resplit a pair
- Surrender is not allowed

Not being a copyrighted game, the other rules vary somewhat from casino to casino. For instance, the dealer may or may not hit a soft 17, or the player may or may not double down after splitting. In most casinos, when both the player and dealer have naturals, the player wins. Depending on which rules are in effect, the house edge can range from 0.7% to 1%. Avoid any game in which a simultaneous player/dealer natural is a push, as it will drive the house edge to over 1.5%

Because of the rule variations, the exact playing strategy that was developed by Stanford Wong takes as many as six charts to describe. Thinking that very few readers would want to tackle such a memorization project, I combined Mr. Wong's charts into a single strategy chart. Of course, I had to make some compromises, so the combined chart is not as accurate as the individual charts, but I believe the difference is relatively insignificant.

As you can see on the next page, the Double Exposure Strategy chart covers a two-page spread.

Note for reading this chart:
• Dealer hands that total less than 4 are always soft hands (A-A, A-2).

• The dealer must stand on any soft hand higher than A 6 so such a hand should be played like a hard 18, 19, or 20. So, play dealer's hands of A7 through A9 the same as hard dealer's 18-20.

Key to chart abbreviations:
S = stand   H = hit   P = split pair
Ds = double down if allowed, else stand
Dh = double down if allowed, else hit
P/S = split if allowed to double after splitting, else stand
P/H = split if allowed to double after splitting, else hit
P/D = split if allowed to double after splitting, else double

DOUBLE EXPOSURE STRATEGY

Player's Hand — Dealer's Upcard

Player's Hand	4	5	6	7	8	9	10	11	12	13	14
A-A	P	P	P	P	P	P	P	H	P	P	P
10-10	S	S	S	S	S	S	S	S	S	P	P
9-9	P	P	P	S	P	S	S	S	P	P	P
8-8	P	P	P	P	P	S	S	S	P	P	P
7-7	P/S	P	P	H	H	H	H	S	P	P	P
6-6	P	P	P	H	H	H	H	H	P	P	P
5-5	Dh	Dh	Dh	Dh	Dh	H	H	H	Dh	Dh	Dh
4-4	H	H	H	H	H	H	H	H	P	P	P
3-3	P/H	P/H	P	H	H	H	H	H	P	P	P
2-2	P/H	P/H	P	H	H	H	H	H	P	P	P
21(A-10)	S	S	S	S	S	S	S	S	S	S	S
20 (A-9)	S	S	S	S	S	S	S	S	S	Ds	Ds
19 (A-8)	S	S	S	S	S	S	S	S	Ds	Ds	Ds
18 (A-7)	Ds	Ds	Ds	S	H	H	H	H	Ds	Dh	Dh
17 (A-6)	H	Dh	Dh	H	H	H	H	H	Dh	Dh	Dh
16 (A-5)	H	Dh	Dh	H	H	H	H	H	Dh	Dh	Dh
15 (A-4)	H	H	Dh	H	H	H	H	H	Dh	Dh	Dh
14 (A-3)	H	H	H	H	H	H	H	H	Dh	Dh	Dh
13 (A-2)	H	H	H	H	H	H	H	H	Dh	Dh	Dh
21	S	S	S	S	S	S	S	S	S	S	S
20	S	S	S	S	S	S	S	S	S	S	S
19	S	S	S	S	S	S	S	S	S	S	S
18	S	S	S	S	S	S	S	S	S	S	S
17	S	S	S	S	S	S	S	S	S	S	S
16	S	S	S	H	S	S	S	S	S	S	S
15	S	S	S	H	H	H	S	S	S	S	S
14	S	S	S	H	H	H	S	S	S	S	S
13	S	S	S	H	H	H	H	S	S	S	S
12	S	S	S	H	H	H	H	H	S	S	S
11	Dh	Dh	Dh	Dh	Dh	Dh	H	H	Dh	Dh	Dh
10	Dh	Dh	Dh	Dh	Dh	H	H	H	Dh	Dh	Dh
9	H	Dh	Dh	H	H	H	H	H	Dh	Dh	Dh
8	H	H	H	H	H	H	H	H	Dh	Dh	Dh
5-7	H	H	H	H	H	H	H	H	H	H	Dh

DOUBLE EXPOSURE STRATEGY

Player's Hand	Dealer's Upcard											
	15	16	17	18	19	20	AA	A2	A3	A4	A5	A6
A-A	P	P	H	H	H	H	P	P	P	P	P	P
10-10	P	P	S	S	S	H	S	S	S	S	S	S
9-9	P	P	S	P	H	H	S	S	S	S	S	S
8-8	P	P	P	H	H	H	S	S	S	S	P	P
7-7	P	P	P	H	H	H	S	S	S	S	S	H
6-6	P	P	P	H	H	H	H	H	S	S	S	H
5-5	Dh	P/D	H	H	H	H	H	H	Dh	Dh	Dh	H
4-4	P	P	H	H	H	H	H	H	H	H	H	H
3-3	P	P	P	H	H	H	H	H	H	H	H	H
2-2	P	P	P	H	H	H	H	H	H	H	H	H
21(A-10)	S	S	S	S	S	S	S	S	S	S	S	S
20 (A-9)	Ds	Ds	S	S	S	H	S	S	S	S	S	S
19 (A-8)	Ds	Ds	S	S	H	H	S	S	S	S	S	S
18 (A-7)	Dh	Dh	S	H	H	H	H	H	H	H	S	S
17 (A-6)	Dh	Dh	H	H	H	H	H	H	H	H	H	H
16 (A-5)	Dh	Dh	H	H	H	H	H	H	H	H	H	H
15 (A-4)	Dh	Dh	H	H	H	H	H	H	H	H	H	H
14 (A-3)	Dh	Dh	H	H	H	H	H	H	H	H	H	H
13 (A-2)	Dh	Dh	H	H	H	H	H	H	H	H	H	H
21	S	S	S	S	S	S	S	S	S	S	S	S
20	S	S	S	S	S	H	S	S	S	S	S	S
19	S	S	S	S	H	H	S	S	S	S	S	S
18	S	S	S	H	H	H	S	S	S	S	S	S
17	S	S	H	H	H	H	S	S	S	S	S	H
16	S	S	H	H	H	H	S	S	S	S	S	H
15	S	S	H	H	H	H	S	S	S	S	S	H
14	S	S	H	H	H	H	S	S	S	S	S	H
13	S	S	H	H	H	H	S	S	S	S	S	H
12	S	S	H	H	H	H	H	H	S	S	S	H
11	Dh	Dh	H	H	H	H	H	Dh	Dh	Dh	Dh	H
10	Dh	Dh	H	H	H	H	H	H	Dh	Dh	Dh	H
9	Dh	Dh	H	H	H	H	H	H	H	H	H	H
8	Dh	Dh	H	H	H	H	H	H	H	H	H	H
5-7	Dh	Dh	H	H	H	H	H	H	H	H	H	H

14

SPANISH 21

Spanish 21 is a computer-derived modification of blackjack that can be found in most of the larger casinos around the country. The term "Spanish" refers to the 48-card deck used in some Spanish card games. It is a regular 52-card deck with the four tens removed. Although, in most respects, Spanish 21 is played just like standard blackjack, the basic strategy is somewhat different.

As a specially-designed version of blackjack, Spanish 21 has liberalized rules and unique bonuses. The casinos can be so generous because removal of the four tens from the deck gives the house a huge advantage. The liberal rules and bonus payouts were designed to attract jaded blackjack players and are what has made the game so popular. For instance, in standard blackjack, it is always exhilarating to reach a count of 21, but it quickly turns into a disappointment if the dealer also gets a 21 (resulting in a push instead of a win). In Spanish 21, if both dealer and player have a total count of 21, the player wins!

Except for the extra bonuses, the game appears to be almost identical to standard blackjack. What fools some experienced blackjack players is that the basic strategy for standard blackjack is less accurate. To keep from losing your shirt, you should learn a modified strategy. When you use the correct strategy, the house edge is about the same as for standard multiple deck blackjack.

WHAT ARE THE RULE DIFFERENCES?

Spanish 21 is played just like standard blackjack, with the following changes and exceptions.

The Deck

The 48-card deck used in Spanish 21 is standard except for the tens that were removed. Removing the tens effectively reduces the number of ten-value cards by 25 percent, giving the dealer a major mathematical advantage. Six or eight of these 48-card decks are shuffled together and dealt from a regular blackjack shoe.

Face Cards

Each face card (jack, queen, and king) has a numerical value of 10. In a standard blackjack deck, there are 16 ten-value cards, while in a Spanish 21 deck, there are only 12 ten-value cards. As a result, the dealer will bust less often and the players will make blackjacks less often. Since the effectiveness of doubling down depends on the prevalence of 10-value cards, its value to the player has been somewhat degraded.

Natural

Whenever you get a natural, you win regardless of what the dealer has, and are paid 3 to 2 odds. This is a nice improvement over standard blackjack where, if you match the dealer's natural, it is just a push. In Spanish 21, you will be dealt an average of one natural in about twenty-four hands. This is not quite as good as standard six- or eight-deck blackjack, where you can expect to get one natural in about twenty-one hands.

21 Count

If your hand reaches a count of 21, you win even odds, even if the dealer gets a 21. You can only lose is if the dealer has a natural. There are no pushes on a 21 hand. Certain card combinations that add up to 21 pay better than even odds. This is covered in the section on bonuses.

Resplit

You may split cards of the same rank up to four times.

Double Down

You may double down on any hand and at any time: on your original two-card hand, after you have taken one or more hits, or after a split. When you double down, however, that hand does not qualify for a bonus.

Double Down Rescue

After getting a double down card, if you don't like the resulting hand, you may take back (rescue) the doubled portion of your wager and forfeit your original bet. This can only be done if the hand did not bust. Assuming you used proper doubling strategy in the first place, this is never a recommended option.

Surrender

Surrender is allowed; the standard rules apply.

SPANISH 21 BONUSES
Bonus 21

Certain non-doubled 21 hands pay bonuses as high as 3 to 1. The bonuses are always paid except when the dealer has a natural. The bonus hands are shown in the following chart:

BONUS 21 PAYTABLE	
HAND	**PAYS**
Five-card 21	3 to 2
Six-card 21	2 to 1
Seven-card 21	3 to 1
6-7-8 Mixed suits	3 to 2
6-7-8 Suited	2 to 1
6-7-8 Spades	3 to 1
7-7-7 Mixed suits	3 to 2
7-7-7 Suited	2 to 1
7-7-7 Spades	3 to 1

The bonuses were carefully designed to get you to take hits that risk busting your hand. To get the bonus for the five, six, or seven card hands, the count has to be exactly 21. You will find that this is not an easy task to accomplish because of the very high probability of busting. If you have the start of a 6-7-8 or 7-7-7 hand and are trying for the bonus, you may have to take a hit when you don't want to.

Super Bonus

When you get a 7-7-7 hand, all of the same suit, *and* the dealer's upcard is a seven of any suit, you will be paid a super bonus and all other players at the table will be paid an "envy" bonus. If you wagered $5 to $24, the super bonus pays $1000. If you bet $25 or more, the super bonus is $5000. In either case, an envy bonus of $50 is paid to every other player at the table. *The super and envy bonuses do not pay off if your hand was split or doubled.*

In some casinos the super bonus payoff is handled differently. You get $1000 for each $5 bet increment, up to a maximum of $5000 for a $25 bet. For instance, if you wagered $15, the bonus would be $3000. Regardless of the wager, the other players still get a $50 envy bonus.

SPANISH 21 STRATEGY

Although the Spanish 21 strategy is similar to the basic strategy for standard blackjack, there are significant differences that should not be overlooked. These differences are mainly due to the twenty-five percent fewer 10-value cards in the deck. The bonuses for certain 21-count hands also contribute to the alteration in strategy rules.

The Spanish 21 strategy chart that is shown on the next page is a consolidated chart derived from strategy that was originally developed by the late Lenny Frome and subsequently refined by Michael Shackleford. When you apply this chart, keep in mind that a soft hand of more than two cards is one in which the ace is counted as an 11. If the ace must be counted as 1 to keep from busting, then it is a hard hand.

In most Spanish 21 games, the dealer must hit a soft 17, thus the main chart, designated as Chart 1, is based on that rule. Occasionally you may be fortunate enough to encounter a game in which the dealer stands on soft 17, in which case Chart 2 shows the differences in strategy.

SPANISH 21 STRATEGY
Chart 1
• Dealer Hits Soft 17 •

Player's Hand	Dealer's Upcard									
	2	3	4	5	6	7	8	9	Face	A
A-A	P	P	P	P	P	P	P	P	P	P
10-10	S	S	S	S	S	S	S	S	S	S
9-9	S	P	P	P	P	S	P	P	S	S
8-8	P	P	P	P	P	P	P	P	P	F
7-7	P	P	P	P	P	Ph	H	H	H	H
6-6	H	H	P	P	P	H	H	H	H	H
5-5	D5	D5	D	D	D	D4	D3	H	H	H
4-4	H	H	H	H	H	H	H	H	H	H
3-3	P	P	P	P	P	P	P	H	H	H
2-2	P	P	P	P	P	P	H	H	H	H
A-9, A-10	S	S	S	S	S	S	S	S	S	S
A-8	S	S	S	S	S	S	S	S	S6	S6
A-7	S4	S4	D4	D5	D6	S6	S4	H	H	H
A-6	H	H	D3	D4	D5	H	H	H	H	H
A-5	H	H	H	D3	D4	H	H	H	H	H
A-4	H	H	H	H	D4	H	H	H	H	H
A-3, A-2	H	H	H	H	H	H	H	H	H	H
18 - 21	S	S	S	S	S	S	S	S	S	S
17	S	S	S	S	S	S	S6	S6	S6	F
16	S6	S6	S6	S	S	H	H	H	H	F
15	S4a	S5b	S6	S6	S	H	H	H	H	H
14	H	H	S4a	S5b	S6c	H	H	H	H	H
13	H	H	H	H	S4a	H	H	H	H	H
12	H	H	H	H	H	H	H	H	H	H
11	D4	D5	D5	D5	D5	D4	D4	D4	D3	D3
10	D5	D5	D	D	D	D4	D3	H	H	H
9	H	H	H	H	D	H	H	H	H	H
5 - 8	H	H	H	H	H	H	H	H	H	H

SPANISH 21 STRATEGY
Chart 2
Differs from Chart 1 when
• Dealer Stands On Soft 17 •

Player's Hand	Dealer's Upcard									
	2	3	4	5	6	7	8	9	Face	A
Pair										
8-8										P
Soft										
19										S
18					D5					
16			H							
15				H						
Hard										
16	S5	S5a								H
15			S5c		S6					
14				S5a	S4a					
13					H					
9					D3					

Key to Chart 1 and Chart 2 abbreviations:
S = stand   H = hit   P = split pair   D = double down
S4, S5, S6 = stand, hit if hand has 4, 5, 6 or more cards
D3, D4, D5, D6 = double, hit if hand has 3, 4, 5, 6
 or more cards
F = surrender on first two cards, otherwise hit
Ph = split, except hit if sevens are suited
a = hit if any 6-7-8 bonus is possible
b = hit if a suited 6-7-8 bonus is possible
c = hit if a spaded 6-7-8 bonus is possible

15

SUPER FUN 21

Super Fun 21 is a copyrighted modification of single-deck blackjack that is found in many casinos. I am including this game because you will encounter it so often in the casinos that one day you may decide to give it a try. Be forewarned, however, that the house edge is higher than for most multiple deck blackjack games.

The lures in this game are the many liberal rules. They are offset, however, by paying only even money on almost all naturals. Most rules are the same as standard blackjack except for the following:

• You may double down on any number of cards, even after splitting and hitting.
• You may split pairs up to three times, including aces.
• You may surrender on any number of cards, even after splitting, hitting, or doubling down.
• A hand totaling 20 or less with six cards and without doubling down, is an automatic winner.
• A hand totaling exactly 21 with five cards or more and without doubling down, is an automatic winner and pays 2 to 1.
• A player's natural is an automatic winner.
• A natural in diamonds pays 2 to 1; other naturals pay even money.

Following is the complete Super Fun 21 strategy chart. This strategy was developed by Michael Shackleford, who calculated the overall house edge to be 0.94%.

Key to chart abbreviations:
S = stand   H = hit   P = split pair   D = double down
S3, S4, S5 = stand, except hit if hand has 3, 4, 5 or more cards
D3, D4, D5 = double, except hit if hand has 3, 4, 5 or more cards
F = surrender

SUPER FUN 21 STRATEGY

Player's Hand	Dealer's Upcard									
	2	3	4	5	6	7	8	9	10	Ace
A-A	P	P	P	P	P	P	P	P	P	P
10-10	S	S	S	S	S	S	S	S	S	S
9-9	S	P	P	P	P	S	P	P	S	P
8-8	P	P	P	P	P	P	P	P	P	P
7-7	P	P	P	P	P	P	P	H	F	F
6-6	P	P	P	P	P	P	H	H	H	H
5-5	D	D	D	D	D	D	D	D	D	D
4-4	H	H	H	P	P	H	H	H	H	H
3-3	P	P	P	P	P	P	H	H	H	H
2-2	P	P	P	P	P	P	H	H	H	H
A-10	S	S	S	S	S	S	S	S	S	S
A-9	S5	S5	S5	S5	S5	S5	S5	S5	S5	S5
A-8	S5	S5	S5	S5	D5	S5	S5	S5	S4	S5
A-7	S3	D4	D4	D4	D5	S4	S4	H	H	H
A-6	D3	D3	D4	D4	D5	H	H	H	H	H
A-5	H	H	D3	D4	D4	H	H	H	H	H
A-4	H	H	D3	D4	D4	H	H	H	H	H
A-3	H	H	D3	D	D	H	H	H	H	H
A-3	H	H	H	D	D	H	H	H	H	H
18 - 21	S	S	S	S	S	S	S	S	S	S
17	S	S	S	S	S	S	S	S5	S5	F5
16	S	S	S	S	S	H	H	H	F4	F4
15	S5	S5	S	S	S	H	H	H	H	F4
14	S5	S5	S5	S5	S5	H	H	H	H	H
13	S4	S4	S5	S5	S5	H	H	H	H	H
12	H	H	S4	S4	S4	H	H	H	H	H
11	D4	D4	D4	D4	D4	D4	D4	D4	D4	D4
10	D4	D4	D4	D4	D4	D4	D4	D4	D3	D4
9	D3	D4	D4	D	D	H	H	H	H	H
5 - 8	H	H	H	H	H	H	H	H	H	H

16

PRIVATE AND HOME BLACKJACK GAMES

In one form or another, more blackjack is played in hotel rooms, in back rooms, in homes, and in military barracks than in legal casinos. Outside of the casinos, blackjack takes on one of two forms: privately-banked games and informal unbanked home games.

PRIVATELY-BANKED GAMES

Privately-banked games are usually of the underground floating variety, where a sponsor operates and banks the game. The sponsor is often a professional gambler who operates the "house" and provides the location, the playing equipment, a professional dealer, food and refreshments, as well as other services. Some of these games are played on a weekly basis, with the location changing from week to week. Many, however, operate five or six days per week.

In most respects, they are just like blackjack games in Las Vegas, except that they are illegal. Typically, they are single-deck hand-dealt games with favorable rules. Consequently, a player can effectively apply the Universal Basic Strategy. The minimum betting limit is usually at least $25, and you often have to show a certain minimum bankroll before you are allowed to play. The main disadvantage to illegal privately-banked games is that many of them are dishonest. Unless you are personally familiar with the sponsors, or the operation has an established reputation for honesty, you would be well advised to avoid such a game.

UNBANKED HOME GAMES

These are the games you played in the barracks while you served your country, or at a friend's or neighbor's house. As the name implies, there is no operator or house to bank the game. These are the games where the deal rotates from player to player, the dealer wins ties, and a natural is paid off at 2 to 1. Obviously, the playing strategy under these rules has to be different than for casino games. Typical rules for unbanked home blackjack games are as follows:

UNBANKED HOME GAME BLACKJACK RULES
1. Single deck
2. Dealer wins ties
3. Natural pays 2 to 1
4. Five-card automatic win
5. Splitting pairs allowed
6. Split aces get one card
7. Double down allowed
8. No insurance offered
9. No surrender offered

With the dealer winning all ties, dealing the game is a big advantage. Even when paying 2 to 1 on naturals, the dealer has an enormous 6.5% advantage over basic strategy players. Against players who do not know basic strategy, the dealer's edge is even greater. By learning the special house game strategy in this chapter, you can cut the dealer's edge to below 5%.

The game usually begins with all players cutting for the high card to see who gets the first deal. In most games, everyone's cards are dealt one face up and one face down. Since the dealer is not constrained by any house playing rules, seeing a player's upcard is a further advantage. To eliminate this advantage, in some games both player's cards are dealt face down.

In some games, the deal rotates to the left after a certain number of hands. Any player who doesn't want the deal may immediately pass it to his left. Why would anyone turn down the deal? Because, if there is a large number of players, you have to have an ample bankroll and be willing to risk it.

In most games, however, any player with a natural can take the deal, provided the dealer didn't also get a natural. If more than one player gets a natural at the same time, the one nearest to the dealer's left gets the deal. Should the dealer no longer want the deal, it can be sold to the highest bidder. A statistically-fair price would be 2 to 3 times the average bet. That is, if the average bet is about $10, a fair price for the deal would be $20 to $30.

The best strategy for unbanked home games is to deal as often as possible. When dealing, if you see an obvious situation on the table, such as when a player splits a pair and all of his cards are exposed, play to beat the player's hands. Otherwise, play your hand like a casino dealer, that is, hit on 16 or less, and stand on 17 or higher.

When you are a player, you must use correct playing strategy to limit the dealer's big advantage. The best playing strategy for unbanked home games was developed by the late Julian Braun, and is shown on the next page. The chart does not include the five-card automatic win rule. Under this rule, whenever a player gets five cards without busting, the hand is an automatic winner.

When the five-card rule is in effect, the home game strategy should be modified according to the indicated chart.

MODIFICATIONS FOR FIVE-CARD AUTOMATIC WIN RULE

1. Hit a four-card count of 15 or less
2. Hit a four-card count of 16 or 17 against a dealer 7 or higher
3. Hit a 3-card count of 12 against a dealer 2 or 3
4. Never split a 2-2

Key to chart abbreviations:
H = hit   S = stand   P = split pair
Dh = double down if allowed, else hit
Ds = double down if allowed, else stand

STRATEGY FOR UNBANKED HOME GAMES

Player's Hand	Dealer's Upcard									
	2	3	4	5	6	7	8	9	10	Ace
A-A	P	P	P	P	P	P	P	P	P	P
10-10	S	S	S	S	S	S	S	S	S	S
9-9	P	P	P	P	P	S	P	S	S	S
8-8	P	P	P	P	P	P	P	S	S	H
7-7	S	P	P	P	P	P	H	H	S	H
6-6	S	P	P	P	P	H	H	H	H	H
5-5	Dh	Dh	Dh	Dh	Dh	Dh	Dh	H	H	H
4-4	H	H	H	P	H	H	H	H	H	H
3-3	H	P	P	P	P	H	H	H	H	H
2-2	H	H	P	P	P	H	H	H	H	H
21(A-10)	S	S	S	S	S	S	S	S	S	S
20 (A-9)	S	S	S	S	S	S	S	S	S	S
19 (A-8)	S	S	S	S	S	S	S	S	S	S
18 (A-7)	S	S	Ds	Ds	Ds	S	H	H	H	H
17 (A-6)	H	H	Dh	Dh	Dh	H	H	H	H	H
16 (A-5)	H	H	H	Dh	Dh	H	H	H	H	H
15 (A-4)	H	H	H	Dh	Dh	H	H	H	H	H
14 (A-3)	H	H	H	Dh	Dh	H	H	H	H	H
13 (A-2)	H	H	H	Dh	Dh	H	H	H	H	H
18 - 21	S	S	S	S	S	S	S	S	S	S
17	S	S	S	S	S	S	S	S	S	H
16	S	S	S	S	S	H	H	S	H	H
15	S	S	S	S	S	H	H	S	H	H
14	S	S	S	S	S	H	H	H	H	H
13	S	S	S	S	S	H	H	H	H	H
12	H	H	S	S	S	H	H	H	H	H
11	Dh	Dh	Dh	Dh	Dh	Dh	Dh	Dh	Dh	H
10	Dh	Dh	Dh	Dh	Dh	Dh	Dh	H	H	H
9	H	H	Dh	Dh	Dh	H	H	H	H	H
5 - 8	H	H	H	H	H	H	H	H	H	H

17

ACE — A card that, in blackjack, may be valued either 1 or 11.

ACTION — The total amount that you bet, regardless of wins or losses. If you bet $10 on 50 hands, then your action was $500.

ANCHOR POSITION — See Third base.

BACK COUNTING — The act of counting cards as a spectator without actually playing.

BANK — (a) Money on the table that is used by the dealer to pay winning bets. (b) The casino or the game operator. (c) Any person who covers all the bets in a game.

BANKROLL — The total amount of money that a player has allotted to a gambling session.

BASIC STRATEGY — The best long-term playing decisions for a person who is not tracking or counting cards.

BLACKJACK — See Natural.

BLACKS — Black casino chips with a value of $100 each.

BLEEDER — A paranoid casino supervisor who worries about players winning. Also called a sweater (one who perspires).

BREAK — See Bust.

BURN CARD — A card removed from the top of the deck after a shuffle, and placed in the discard tray.

BUST — To exceed a total count of 21 in blackjack. Also called break.

BUY-IN — (a) An exchange of a player's currency for casino chips. (b) The amount of money a player gives the dealer for the chips.

CAGE — A shortened term for the cashier's cage.

CARD COUNTER — A person who mentally keeps track of the which cards have been played, so as to determine which cards remain in the unplayed deck.

CARD MECHANIC — A skilled dealer who uses sleight-of-hand to cheat.

CHECK OR CHEQUE — Alternate term for Chip that is commonly used by casino personnel and professional gamblers.

CHIP — A gaming token with an imprinted value that is used in place of real money at various table games. Chips may be redeemed for cash at the issuing casino. Also called house check, casino chip, or value chip. The terms Chip and Check are used interchangeably.

GLOSSARY

COMP — A shortening for complementary. The term used for free meals, lodging, and other services provided by the casino to regular players.

CSM — An acronym for Continuous Shuffling Machine. This device speeds up the game by eliminating shuffling delays and completely thwarts card counting.

CUT CARD — A special card, usually solid in color, used to cut the deck.

DEALER — The casino employee who operates the game and deals the cards.

DEUCE — The two-spot card.

DOUBLE DOWN — A rule that allows a player to double his bet and receive one additional card. Also called doubling.

DOUBLE EXPOSURE — A variant of blackjack where both dealer cards are dealt face up.

EARLY SURRENDER — See Surrender.

EDGE — A statistical advantage. Usually the casino's advantage.

EVEN MONEY — A wager that pays off at 1 to 1 odds, if it wins. That is, if a $10 bet wins, the original bet is returned along with an additional $10. Also called a flat bet or even odds.

EXPECTATION — The average amount that may be won or lost in a particular game over an extended period of play. Also called expectation of winning.

FACE CARD — A jack, queen, or king. In blackjack, all face cards have a value of 10.

FACE DOWN CARDS — Cards that are not exposed.

FACE UP CARDS — Cards that are exposed for all to see.

FIRST BASE — The end seat at a gaming table, to the dealer's immediate left, which is the first hand that is dealt and played.

FLOOR SUPERVISOR — A pit supervisor who reports to the pit boss. This is the person who watches dealers to assure that all losing bets are collected, winning bets are correctly paid, and nobody is cheating.

GREENS — Green casino chips with a value of $25 each. Also called quarters.

HAND — The cards held by a player.

HARD HAND — A hand with a total count of 12 or higher that either does not contain an ace or the ace can only be valued as 1, without going over 21.

HIT — A player's decision to draw another card.

GLOSSARY

HOLE CARD — The dealer's face down card.

HOUSE — The casino, the bank, or the game operator.

HOUSE EDGE — The difference between the actual odds and the payoff odds, usually stated as a percentage, which is the mathematical edge the house has over the player. Also called casino advantage, house percentage, or P.C.

HOUSE ODDS — The amount the house pays a winning bet, usually stated as an odds ratio such as 2 to 1. Also called odds paid or payoff odds.

INSURANCE — A side bet on whether or not the dealer has a natural when an ace is showing.

LATE SURRENDER — See Surrender.

LAYOUT — The imprinted surface of a gaming table displaying the positions of the bets.

LIMIT — See Table limit.

MARKER — A casino IOU which permits a player to obtain chips against his established credit or money on deposit.

MAXIMUM — See Table limit.

MINIMUM — The smallest bet allowed at a table.

NATURAL — An initial hand consisting of an ace and a ten-value card. Also called blackjack.

NICKELS — See Reds.

ODDS — The ratio of the number of ways to win versus the number of ways to lose.

ODDS PAID — See House odds.

PAIR — Two cards of the same value, such as a 5-5 or a 9-9. In blackjack, a pair may be split and played as two separate hands. In most casinos, unlike ten-value cards, such as a jack and a king may be split.

PAT HAND — A good hand, that does not require a draw or a hit. In blackjack, it is an unbusted hand with a total count of 17 or higher.

PAYOFF — The amount paid for a winning hand.

PAYOUT — Same as *payoff*.

PAYOFF ODDS — See House odds.

P.C. — Gambler's abbreviation for percentage. See House edge.

PIT — The area behind a group of gaming tables that is restricted to casino employees.

PIT BOSS — The supervisor who is responsible for the tables in a specific pit or gaming area. The pit boss reports to the shift manager.

PUSH — A tie between a player and the dealer in which no money changes hands.

QUARTERS — See Greens.

REDS — Red casino chips with a value of $5 each. Also called nickels.

SHOE — A box, at a dealer's left side, that holds several decks of shuffled cards that can be dealt out one at a time.

SIDE BET — An optional second bet at a table game.

SOFT HAND — A hand containing an ace that can be valued as an 11 without going over 21.

SPLIT — A rule that allows a player to divide a pair into two separate hands.

STAND — A player's decision to not draw any additional cards.

STIFF HAND — A hand that is not pat and can be busted with a single hit. In blackjack, it is a hand with a total count of 12 through 16.

SURRENDER — An option to drop out of play before taking a hit in return for forfeiting half the original wager. The term almost always refers to *late surrender* in which the option is not available until after the dealer checks for a natural. At one time, *early surrender* was offered, allowing the player to surrender before the dealer checked for a natural.

TABLE LIMIT — The largest bet allowed at a table, which may be increased for a high roller. Also called limit or maximum.

THIRD BASE — The end seat at a gaming table, to the dealer's right, which is the last hand that is dealt and played. Also called *anchor position.*

TOKE — Short for token, a gratuity given to the dealer. To comply with IRS rulings, tips are placed into toke boxes and periodically divided between all the dealers, after taxes have been withheld.

TWENTY-ONE — Another term for the game of blackjack.

UPCARD — A card that is dealt face up.

BACCARAT MASTER CARD COUNTER
New Winning Strategy!

For the **first time**, GRI releases the **latest winning techniques** for making money at baccarat. This **exciting copyrighted** strategy, played by **big money players** in Monte Carlo and other exclusive locations, is **not available anywhere else.** Based on the same principles that have made insiders and pros **hundreds of thousands of dollars** at blackjack—card counting!

MATHEMATICALLY TESTED
Filled with charts for **easy reference and understanding**. Contains the most thorough mathematical **analysis** of baccarat in print (though explained in terms anyone can understand). You'll see exactly how this strategy works.

SIMPLE TO USE, EASY TO MASTER
You'll learn how to count cards without the mental effort needed for blackjack! No need to memorize numbers—keep the count on the scorepad. Easy-to-use, play the strategy while enjoying the game!

LEARN WHEN TO BET BANKER, PLAYER
No more hunch bets—use the *Baccarat Master Card Counter* to determine **when to bet Player or Banker**. You learn the basic counts (running and true), deck favorability, symmetrical vs. non-symmetrical play, when to increase bets and much **more** in this **winning strategy**.

PLAY SCIENTIFICALLY TO WIN
Drawing and standing advantage, average edge, average gain, total gain, win-loss and % of occurrence are shown for every relevant hand. You won't need to know these numbers or percentages, but we've included them here so you see exactly how the strategy works. You'll be the best player at the table—after just one reading! Baccarat can be beaten. This strategy shows you how!

This copyrighted strategy can only be purchased from Cardoza Publishing

To order send just $50 by check or money order to:
Cardoza Publishing, P.O. Box 98115, Las Vegas, NV 89193

SERIOUS BLACKJACK TITLES
BOOKS YOU MUST HAVE

THE BLACKJACK
SHUFFLE TRACKER'S COOKBOOK
by Arnold Snyder
$49.95

In this 110-page professional report, Arnold Snyder reveals techniques never-before disclosed on the advanced and dangerous form of card counting known as shuffle tracking. These powerful techniques, known only to a few professional players, are way below the casino radar and allows players to use their winning skills long before the casinos ever get wind that there is an advantage player taking their money.

Included are numerous practice and testing methods for learning shuffle tracking, methods for analyzing and comparing the profit potential of various shuffles, the cost of errors; and much, much more. The hard data is organized into simple charts, and carefully explained. Note: If you are not currently a card counter, this book is not the place to start as shuffle tracking is not easy. This is for serious players only.

THE CARD COUNTER'S GUIDE TO CASINO
SURVEILLANCE
by D.V. Cellini
$99.99

Learning the subtleties of playing winning blackjack undetected is an extremely difficult skill. It's hard enough to fool the casino employees you can see—dealers, floormen, pit bosses, and casino managers—but then there's the "eye," the behind-the-scenes surveillance department, with its biometric-identifying software along with the surveillance agents themselves. But now, for the first time ever, a long-time surveillance agent with vast experience and knowledge has emerged from the deep and dark recesses and exposed the inner workings to the light of scrutiny.

This 135-page special report is packed with inside advice on solo and team-play tactics; how to fly below the radar screen; how to confuse the agents and software; successful camouflage and counter-offensive techniques; and even sure-fire ways to get busted. This is a mighty weapon in any card-counter's arsenal—and it's fascinating reading for anyone interested in how casinos really work.

Win at Blackjack Without Counting Cards!!!

Multiple Deck 1, 2, 3 Non-Counter - Breakthrough in Blackjack!!!

BEAT MULTIPLE DECK BLACKJACK WITHOUT COUNTING CARDS!

You heard right! Now, for the **first time ever**, win at multiple deck blackjack **without counting cards**! Until I developed the Cardoza Multiple Deck Non-Counter (the 1,2,3 Strategy), I thought it was impossible. Don't be intimidated anymore by four, six or eight deck games—for **you have the advantage**. It doesn't matter how many decks they use, for this easy-to-use and proven strategy keeps you **winning—with the odds**!

EXCITING STRATEGY—ANYONE CAN WIN! - We're **excited** about this strategy
for it allows anyone at all, against any number of decks, to have the **advantage** over any casino in the world in a multiple deck game. You don't count cards, you don't need a great memory, you don't need to be good at math - you just need to know the **winning secrets** of the 1,2,3 Multiple Deck Non-Counter and use but a **little effort** to win $$$.

SIMPLE BUT EFFECTIVE! - Now the answer is here. This strategy is so **simple**, yet
so **effective**, you will be amazed. With a **minimum of effort**, this remarkable strategy, which we also call the 1,2,3 (as easy as 1,2,3), allows you to win without studiously following cards. Drink, converse with your fellow players or dealer - they'll never suspect that you can **beat the casino**!

PERSONAL GUARANTEE - And you have my personal **guarantee of satisfaction**,
100% money back! This breakthrough strategy is my personal research and is guaranteed to give you the edge! If for any reason you're not satisfied, send back the materials unused within 30 days for a full refund.

BE A LEISURELY WINNER! - If you just want to play a **leisurely game** yet have the
expectation of winning, the answer is here. Not as powerful as a card counting strategy, but **powerful enough to make you a winner** - with the odds!!!

EXTRA BONUS! - Complete listing of all options and variations at blackjack and how
they affect the player. ($5.00 Value!)

EXTRA, EXTRA BONUS!! - Not really a bonus since we can't sell you the strategy
without protecting you against getting barred. The 1,000 word essay, "How to Disguise the Fact That You're an Expert," and the 1,500 word "How Not To Get Barred," are also included free. ($15.00 Value)

To order, send ~~$75~~ $50 (plus postage and handling) by check or money order to:
Cardoza Publishing, P.O. Box 98115, Las Vegas, NV 89193

$25 OFF! (Only $50 With This Coupon!)

Yes! I want to be a winner at blackjack! Please rush me the **Cardoza Multiple Deck Non-Counter** (The **1,2,3 Strategy**). I understand that all the two bonus essays, and the "Options and Variations" Charts all will be included **absolutely free**! Enclosed is a check or money order for $50 (plus postage and handling) made out to:

Cardoza Publishing, P.O. Box 98115, Las Vegas, NV 89193

MC/Visa/Amex Orders Toll-Free in U.S. & Canada, 1-800-577-WINS

Include $5.00 postage/handling for U.S. orders; $10.00 for Can/Mex; HI/AK and other countries $15.00. Outside U.S., money order payable in U.S. dollars on U.S. bank only.

NAME_____

ADDRESS_____

CITY _____ STATE _____ ZIP _____

MC/Visa/Amex Orders By Mail

MC/Visa/Amex # _____ Phone _____

Exp. Date _____ Signature _____

Order Now! 30 Day Money Back Guarantee!

Beat Mult 17